DISCARD

Mommy Rescue Guide

Welcome to the lifesaving *Mommy Rescue Guide* series! Each *Mommy Rescue Guide* offers techniques and advice written by recognized parenting authorities.

These engaging, informative books give you the help you need when you need it the most! The *Mommy Rescue Guides* are quick, issue-specific, and easy to carry anywhere and everywhere.

You can read one from cover to cover or just pick out the information you need for rapid relief! Whether you're in a bind or you have some time, these books will make being a mom painless and fun!

Being a good mom has never been easier!

Contents

Introduction

As a new mommy, you're bound to have plenty of questions. How do I breastfeed my baby? Should I use cloth diapers or disposable diapers? How do I know when it's time to start my baby on solid foods, and what developmental milestones should I be looking for, and when?

First of all, you're not alone! All moms ask these questions and more, but don't worry—the *Mommy Rescue Guide: Baby's First Year* is here to help. This collection of information gathered from pediatricians, doulas, midwives, and—most importantly—experienced moms is a resource that will enable you to be the great mom you are.

With practical, up-to-date information and plenty of wisdom from real-life experience, this book will help you become familiar with all things baby!

While this book addresses the many speed bumps you'll encounter over this first exciting year of life with your baby, this book isn't just about tackling the challenges of taking care of a new little person. It's about enjoying the first year as a unique and wonderful time to spend with your baby as you watch her take her first wobbly steps, master the art of eating finger foods, and start exploring our great big world. During this special year, know that the *Mommy Rescue Guide: Baby's First Year* will give you direction and support along the way. Enjoy it!

Chapter 1

Welcome Home! Adjusting to Your New Family

THE NURSES AND MIDWIVES gave me lots of advice as I was leaving the hospital, most of which I didn't remember. However, there was one important rule I did follow: "When you get home," my midwife told me, "change immediately into a nightgown and robe, and don't put on regular clothes for seven days."

Settling in with Your Baby

My husband and I left San Francisco's Children's Hospital at 9 P.M. on a Saturday night, some forty-five hours after my first son was born, three hours before our insurance coverage would have expired. It took us about half an hour to fumble tiny Alexander into his going-home sleeper, and almost as long to figure out how to adjust the car seat and strap him into it. The strangest part, however, was walking into our empty house, having left it only two days earlier, with the sense that so much had changed. Once we figured out how to get Alexander out of the car seat, we weren't sure we knew exactly what to do with him.

That awareness of yourselves as new parents sets the stage for how you are going to handle the job of parenting and relating to your child. As nice as it might be, do not have relatives come and stay in your house for the first week after you bring your first baby home. This is an important time for parent/infant bonding, and privacy is necessary for the parents to develop competence and confidence.

Gifts for Mom

Your family and friends may ask what they can do to help. The best gifts during these early weeks may be daytime visitors who come in, do some cleaning, cooking, and laundry, and then quietly go home or back to their hotel. Ask someone to take the older children out for an afternoon, or bring in a home-cooked meal. (Roasted turkey is perfect for hot or cold leftovers, bone picking, and soup.) Other great gifts are a cordless phone to keep near the nursery or gift certificates to local restaurants that offer take out.

Whether it's going to the post office, dry cleaner, or video store, someone else can do your errands. Once you know that your house and home are being cared for, you'll be able to relax. Then you'll have time to enjoy your flowers, look at the cards and bouquets that are delivered, and think about all the people who love you and your baby.

Rules for Your First Week at Home

Your partner will have to help you out here, but this is the time to concentrate on yourselves and your family. Rest and privacy are necessary for both your and your infant's well-being.

There are a bunch of little things that you can do to make yourself more comfortable. For example, in case some people may not have heard, record a baby announcement on your answering machine, and then unplug the phone. Also, don't sit down without something to drink in front of you—especially if you're breastfeeding. It's important to stay well hydrated, for your sake and your baby's. And you should try to take at least two naps a day.

Try to limit your visiting hours. Friends and neighbors may come bearing gifts or food. Graciously thank them, explain that you're too tired for company, and say you look forward to seeing them over the next several weeks.

The best way to ensure that you do rest and spend time alone with your baby is to stay in your nightgown and robe. Living in a nightgown for a week (I had two that would work for nursing and just kept washing them) has several purposes. First of all, it

Mommy Must

In order to politely preserve quiet and privacy, hang a simple note on your front door explaining that mom and her new baby are sleeping. Ask the person not to knock or ring, but let them know where they can leave deliveries.

reminds you—and everyone else—that the most important thing you can do for yourself at this point is rest and let other people take care of you. You're a lot less likely to want to do chores around the house or run an errand if you're in your nightgown, and people (like your partner) are less likely to expect you to do anything more than feed your baby. (Someone else should be changing the diapers for now.)

Healing at Home

Whether you had a vaginal or C-section delivery, it is common for you to go home still feeling some pain—but there are ways to make yourself feel better! First, ask your partner to keep those ice packs coming. Or find a discrete patch of sun and expose your perineum for a few minutes a few times a day, which might help it heal more quickly. You can also run a shallow bath or use your sitz bath or baby tub. If you have a rubber donut, use it as a cushion in the bath.

Herbal Baths
When you take a bath, adding an herbal infusion to the water may speed healing. Possibilities include witch hazel or cypress, which are astringents and may stimulate the constriction of blood vessels; and comfrey or lavender, which are thought to be soothing. You can buy these as extracts or as dry herbs that you steep in hot water.

You may be able to find premixed packets of herbs for postpartum healing. One type, labeled "After Birth Sitz Bath Herbs," includes the following ingredients: Comfrey leaves, comfrey root, myrrh gum powder, garlic, sage, sea salt, uva ursi, and shepherd's purse. If you use this, brew it strong, store it in the refrigerator, and add it to the sitz-bath water. You can also drink a cup of comfrey-leaf tea to encourage healing. Making batches of this herbal brew is a great task to pass off to your partner or helpful guests.

More Herbal Remedies for Postpartum Relief

Several of these herbal remedies may provide simple comfort for you now:

- Aloe vera gel (fresh, from a plant) may cool your skin and relieve pain. Squeeze the gel from a leaf onto your sanitary pad.
- Ginger may soothe stitches from a cesarean. Soak a clean cloth compress in an infusion made of boiled water and grated ginger.
- Golden seal infusion might prevent infection and relieve pain. Use it in a sitz bath.
- Slippery elm bark is thought to soothe pain from perinea tears and strengthen the skin. Make a paste combining the powder, water, and olive oil and spread directly on tear.

Getting Used to Your New Body

As I've said before, your priority during these first days is getting enough rest. The only way you can recover physically, establish your milk supply, and bond with your baby is if you are well rested. This is a special time—preserve it.

It's also time for your body to adjust to its new role. Your hormone levels are shifting and adjusting again, you're healing, you're up at all hours, you're excited, and maybe you're nervous, too. Simply put—you're tired.

Your hormones aren't the only things adjusting themselves. Perryn Rowland, a certified childbirth educator, said, "As a doula [a labor assistant], the most important thing I do for postpartum mothers is help them process the birth experience. This is a major event, and you need to talk about it. You need to reminisce about how you were feeling when this nurse walked in, laugh about how mad you got at your husband, and go over the birth in detail.

"And the dads need to talk about what they were experiencing. Because only after you talk about this tremendous thing that you both went through, only

Mindful Mommy

If you burst into tears, go to bed. If you're still crying after you wake up and you're nervous about postpartum depression, call your healthcare provider; you may need medical help while your hormones slowly return to normal.

after you process the birth, can you move on and meet the next challenge."

Buy a journal or a notebook, or even record your impressions in your baby book. Listening to your partner and seeing your story in your own words will add a whole new dimension to your experience.

Eat Smart—You're Still Eating for Two!

If you're nursing, you need 500 calories a day more than when you were pregnant, just to maintain your weight. For an average woman, that adds up to 2,700 calories a day. Include eight eight-ounce glasses of noncaffeinated fluid. If you drink when you're thirsty and your urine is light in color, you know your fluid intake is adequate.

Keeping up your calcium intake is important as well; you need a total of five glasses of milk or calcium equivalents a day. Insufficient calcium won't affect your milk supply, but your body will raid its own calcium stores to make up the difference, weakening your bones and teeth. (If you keep up your calcium intake after weaning, your bone mass will return.) It doesn't take milk to make breastmilk; if you are allergic to dairy products, eat plenty of green, leafy vegetables and make sure you're getting enough of other fluids.

You may want to avoid gassy foods, such as cabbage and broccoli; these bother some babies. And stick to decaffeinated coffee or limited amounts of regular coffee. The amount of caffeine that gets into breastmilk is small, but do you really want to risk making your baby wake up more often? You can eat all the garlic you want—the flavor does get into your breastmilk and, much to the surprise of the researchers who decided to study this, most babies like the taste and nurse better.

Chapter 2

Getting to Know Sleep Basics for You and Your Baby

WHEN YOU WALK DOWN the street, pushing your baby in a stroller, and stop to exchange coos with another mother, you don't want to know what book she's reading or if she's seen the latest romantic comedy in theaters. You want to know how much her baby sleeps. (And it's probably more than your baby does.)

Sleeping Positions

You have probably been inundated with flyers about back sleeping by now, so I won't belabor this. However, it's important to repeat that the American Academy of Pediatrics (AAP) recommends that healthy infants be placed on their backs to sleep, as recent studies have shown that back sleeping is related to a lower incidence of Sudden Infant Death Syndrome (SIDS). So, you absolutely should put your baby down to sleep on her back; the side sleeping position is a second choice.

Sleep Patterns Explained

When you first bring your baby home from the hospital, she will sleep an average of fifteen hours a day, generally in random chunks throughout the day and night. (Note: Your baby may sleep almost all the time, or as little as eleven hours or less.) Your baby may be at her most alert at 2 A.M. and have no interest in going back to sleep until 4 A.M. This day/night reversal is not unusual. While you were pregnant, your baby probably did a lot of her sleeping during the day, when you were walking around and rocking her with your movements, then got more active as soon as you lay down for the night.

Don't worry, though! You can begin to teach your baby that it's much more fun to be awake during the daytime than it is at night. If your baby was in the nursery at the hospital, day differed little from night—lights on, babies crying, people moving about twenty-four hours a day. At home, though, you can

Mommy Must

Positional plagiocephaly is the flat spot on your baby's head that may develop if she always sleeps in one position. Try to get your baby to vary which side of her head rests on the mattress when she is asleep. During the day when she is awake, make sure you put her down on her stomach occasionally.

make day and night distinct. Try waking your baby up every two hours in the afternoon, and whenever he's awake during the day, make it fun time. Talk to him, get out those baby toys, take him outside to listen to the birds, and introduce him to visitors.

At night, don't talk to him much, don't turn on anything more than a nightlight, don't play with him—don't even change his diaper unless it's dirty or soaking through. In time, most babies will welcome nighttime with their longest chunk of sleep—as much as four or five hours. (Realistically, though, you probably won't go to bed the minute your baby does, so you still won't be getting nearly as much sleep as you need.)

By the end of the third month, she should be doing the bulk of her sleeping at night. (But still not, unfortunately, in long enough stretches to make you feel like you've really slept.)

The Sleep-Deprived Mommy

After three months, the sleep deprivation will start to wear on you, and you will begin to wonder if your baby will ever sleep through the night. The effect of sleep deprivation is much more pronounced than being simply tired. While you'll notice delayed reaction times, clumsiness, and blurred vision, you might be too exhausted to notice impaired reasoning and judgment, apathy and agitation, and an increased sensitivity to pain.

In addition to being forgetful, confused, and increasingly irritable, you will seriously start to resent the mothers of babies who are sleeping 7 P.M. to 7 A.M. (you *will* meet these people), and wonder if you're doing something wrong. You're not. They just drew good cards for this hand and have kids who like to sleep. If you're one of those, you can skip the rest of this section and save your energy for the next challenge your child throws at you. (But try to keep quiet about the amount of sleep you're getting; the rest of us really don't want to hear about it.)

For me, the magic number is five. If I have five consecutive hours of sleep, and a few more hours of interrupted sleep, I am a reasonably sane person. I can remember where I put my car keys, walk without tripping, and usually carry on a rational conversation. But if I go weeks at a time without that five-hour chunk of sleep, I start having problems. When my daughter was a wakeful newborn, I toweled my four-year-old son dry, then struggled mightily to tape a size 1 diaper around him, annoyed because, for some reason, the silly thing didn't fit. I'm not sure why he stood so quietly as I struggled with this—either he

Mommy Knows Best

Turn off the lights when you put your baby to sleep at night. Babies typically don't become afraid of the dark until the age of two, so until then, why start the night-light habit?

was shocked into silence or he was afraid that if he stopped me I might try something really crazy.

So, the issue isn't how much sleep your baby is getting—it's whether you are getting enough hours of sleep to cope as a parent, and how many of those hours are unbroken. Only you know how much "enough" sleep is and how best you can get it. If you are dangerously sleep deprived and your baby will drink from a bottle, try spending an occasional night sleeping (alone) on the couch of a childless friend while your partner handles night duty. One night's rest can make all the difference.

Sleep Strategies You May Consider

Now, can those of us not blessed with sleeping beauties do anything to get our babies to sleep just a little longer? Maybe. There are plenty of programs to pick from; some may work for your new baby, and then not work for your next one. Some may seem remarkably sensible to you, but to someone else they may seem nuts.

Before exploring the different programs, let's look at the relative importance of sleep issues. You may read that it is important for your baby to learn to fall asleep by himself, because learning this will make him self-reliant. Personally, I don't think so. I don't think my kids were less confident about their ability to slither down a slide on their own or had a harder time separating from me on their first days of preschool because I didn't teach them to fall asleep alone by the age of six months.

You may also read that babies will sleep more soundly if alone in a crib, but your baby will get plenty of sleep even if you're sitting up holding her all night. Actually, she'll sleep just great that way.

In addition to structured sleep methods, there are some simple practices that just plain work. Like any method, they won't work for all babies, but they're helpful and may work for yours. When your baby is a newborn, let him fall asleep in your arms, then gently put him down in the bassinet or crib, keeping one hand on his chest the whole time. Place both hands on him for a moment after he's down, then lift them very slowly.

Keeping your baby awake when he's tired during the day will not make him sleep better at night—it will just make him more cranky. Nap timing does have an effect, however, and you'll be much better off if your baby takes an afternoon nap than if he stays awake all afternoon and falls asleep at 5 P.M. Don't worry about building a bad habit in a baby who's under three months old—if it works for tonight, it's good enough!

Using motion is another tried and true method for getting your baby to sleep, so look for anything that keeps your baby rocking or gently bouncing. In addition to a glider or rocker, try holding the baby while bouncing on an exercise ball. Sitting and bouncing will also be more restful for you, and beats pacing the floor.

If you need a hands-free method, a windup swing or vibrating bouncy seat will soothe her to sleep.

Keep her in the kitchen while you're cooking, or rest the seat near a tumbling dryer (but don't leave her without supervision). The constant hum might work on your baby. Get a tape player that reverses automatically, and stock up on cassettes of lullabies or your own favorite soothing tunes.

And if all else fails, there's always driving. Rumbling bumps, a rocking motion, and the running engine combine the best of everything. It can be wildly impractical, or you may find it relaxing—my favorite baby-sleep drive was to the ocean, where, once my baby was asleep, I'd park facing the waves and get out a book.

Personal Sleep Programs

When you're trying to decide what to do about your baby and sleep, consider what will work for your baby. Don't worry that you're stuck once you make your choice. If you're like most of us, you'll try a few methods, settle on one for your first child, and then find that it is completely ineffective for your second child.

Mindful Mommy

If you want your baby to become attached to a lovey (a blanket, stuffed animal, or comfort object other than your skin), nudge her toward something you can buy more than one of (just in case!).

There are a few rules that many—but not all—of the programs share. If you don't want to go all the way with any one approach, you might start with these elements as you work out a system of your own:

- Try to put your baby down to sleep when he is drowsy but awake. This may teach him to put himself back to sleep when he wakes up.
- Establish a prebed ritual and don't vary from it. Make sure it is of a reasonable length and includes books or songs that you won't be tired of for years to come.
- Get your baby attached to a lovey, also known as a transitional object. The idea here is that the baby will look for the lovey when she wants to calm down. Some people do question whether you want your baby to bond with you, the mother, or with a yellow duck, but when you absolutely can't be there, lovies really come in handy.
- Don't do anything. Your baby will eventually sleep through the night—at least sometime before he's a teenager, at which point your problem will be dragging him out of bed before noon.

Learning the Ferber Method

In the program proposed by Richard Ferber in his 1985 book *Solve Your Child's Sleep Problems* (now dubbed "Ferberizing" by moms), the goal is for the baby to learn to put herself to sleep alone in a crib, and then to put herself back to sleep without a fuss when she wakes up during the night. This is meant to be a positive experience that gradually teaches the child to fall back on her own resources for comfort.

Ferber likens the process to what an adult would have to go through should he be forbidden to sleep with a pillow. At first he'd have trouble falling asleep and would wake repeatedly, but, after a few nights, he'd get used to it and sleep just fine.

Ferber's system, like many others, starts with a bedtime ritual (a bath perhaps, followed by a book or a song). You or your partner then put your baby to bed while the baby is still awake. The parent leaves the room (and the baby cries). The parent returns in brief, increasing intervals, such as five, then ten, then fifteen minutes, and at subsequent fifteen-minute intervals to reassure the baby that she has not been abandoned. The parent does not stay in the room, rock the baby, or give her any "crutches" (like a bottle or a pacifier). And, no matter what, the parent does not take the baby out of the crib. This is repeated every time the baby wakes during the night. Starting on the second night, each interval is extended by five minutes or as long as you can tolerate.

While Ferber offers gradual alternatives (sitting next to the crib in a chair, for example, and moving the chair farther away every night), the approach of leaving for timed intervals is the one he most recommends.

Ferberizing may go on for hours a night, for days, or rarely, weeks. It usually works eventually. The big question is whether or not you are able to make it to the "eventually." (In most cases, dads have an easier time sticking to this program; the hormones released in nursing mothers when listening to a screaming baby for an extended period of time do not make things any easier.)

Since Ferber's book came out, a number of similar but slightly modified plans have been published. Probably the best news is that recent research has shown that you don't need to repeat the Ferber process each time the baby wakes up during the night. Do it once at the beginning of the night, and then go ahead and rock him to sleep when he wakes up. In most cases, that won't delay the onset of the era when the baby finally sleeps consistently through the night.

Family Bed: Is It Safe? Does It Work?

Parents, babies, and young siblings sleeping together in the family bed is the way babies have slept throughout most of history—and still do in much of the world. In the United States today, it has been repopularized as one of the tenets of a childrearing philosophy called Attachment Parenting. The family bed is evangelized by William Sears in *Nighttime Parenting* and *The Baby Book*. Sears says that babies sleep differently than adults, with more waking periods and longer periods of light sleep, for a reason— they need to be able to wake easily when they are hungry, cold, or their breathing is compromised.

The family bed has several benefits beyond the closeness and awareness it fosters between you and your baby. You may find it easier to get your baby to sleep on her back, and your sleep cycles will become synchronized. When you do wake up, it will be out of a light sleep rather than a deep one, and soothing or feeding her will be that much easier.

Sears suggests nursing or rocking the baby into a sound sleep before putting him down, either in a cradle or the parents' bed. Whenever the baby wakes up, you should get to the baby quickly, he says, since you'll probably have an easier time getting the baby back to sleep if he doesn't scream himself into hysteria first. Here's where having the baby in bed with you is an advantage—you can often soothe, or even breastfeed, your baby without fully coming awake yourself.

The family bed became controversial in 1999, when the Consumer Products Safety Commission issued a warning against adults sleeping with babies in adult beds. This warning was based on information obtained when the Commission used death certificate data in a study that attempted to identify products associated with infant suffocation. The study

Mommy Knows Best

Putting your baby in a crib has its own benefits. You may find that you sleep better with more room and without a squirming, kicking bundle beside you. If you can't sleep for fear of squishing the baby, or if you have a panic attack every time she makes a noise, you won't sleep at all or function well when you're supposed to be awake.

was criticized for its methodology, most significantly for not taking into account other risk factors, such as parents under the influence of drugs and alcohol, number of babies sleeping on sofas or waterbeds, and number of mothers who smoked during pregnancy or at the time of the baby's death. Despite the criticism, there has been no better study since.

To safely share a bed with your baby:

- Keep the bed away from walls and other furniture (to eliminate the danger of the baby getting trapped on the side of the bed).
- Move pillows away from your baby.
- Don't use a wavy waterbed.
- For comfort, get the biggest bed you can.

Remember: Never sleep with your baby if you have taken any sedative, such as alcohol, over-the-counter cold medications, or narcotics. It's also not a good idea if you smoke. If the label says that you shouldn't be driving or handling heavy machinery when taking the drug, you shouldn't be sleeping with your baby, either.

Focal Feedings

This modified cry-it-out approach is advocated by Joanne Cuthbertson and Susie Schevill, authors of *Helping Your Child Sleep Through the Night*. Their program varies slightly with the age of the child, but basically, it goes like this: Wake up your baby at 11 or 11:30 P.M.—or just before you are ready to go to bed—and feed her. This will theoretically prevent her from waking up an hour or two later to interrupt your deepest sleep.

If you are breastfeeding, have your partner go in when your baby wakes up and try to settle him in his crib without picking him up. If he doesn't fall asleep within ten to twenty minutes, your partner should pick him up, walk him around—anything to distract him for another hour or so before the next feeding. The idea is to get the baby adjusted to longer periods of sleep between awakenings. An alternative is to limit the amount of time the baby nurses in the middle of the night (which can be easier for both of you than not feeding him at all). If you are bottle-feeding, dilute the formula so your baby adjusts to receiving fewer calories overnight.

Scheduled Wakings

In this program, you try to take control of your baby's night wakings. First, you note which times your child typically wakes up, then set an alarm clock to wake you up before she does. Then wake her up, feed her, and put her back to sleep. After she's used to this, start waking her up later and later, the idea being that she'll eventually forget to wake up on her own.

Protect the Sleep Schedule

For every program there seems to be an opposite. Marc Weissbluth, a sleep disorders specialist at Children's Memorial Hospital in Chicago, advocates never waking your baby—never ever, not even if you're late and absolutely have to leave the house. He believes sleep problems are created when parents interrupt their babies' sleep or allow them to get overtired.

When the baby is very young, Weissbluth advocates putting him to sleep after two hours of wakefulness, and doing whatever it takes to achieve this (rocking, singing, pacifier). Your baby may cry in protest; allow the crying to continue from five to twenty minutes, then pick him up and try again. From four to twelve months, try making your baby take two naps a day (never in the car or stroller) and then enforcing an early bedtime. If the baby cries at bedtime, says Weissbluth, do not go in at all, because "down is down."

Now you know several different methods that mommies just like you use to get your baby to sleep for longer periods of time at night. Try to make an informed decision, and if you choose one of the ones listed here, why not get another book all about that method and learn the real ins and outs? Good luck and sleep well!

Chapter 3

Crying Out—What Does It Mean?

WHEN YOUR CHILD IS born, she typically greets the world with a wail. You will probably be thrilled to hear that first cry. This will also probably be the last time you will be happy to hear your baby cry. For the next few years, you'll be putting a lot of effort into getting your child to stop crying.

Infant Crying: What's Your Baby Trying to Say?

The first few days after birth, your baby may do nothing but sleep, and hardly cry at all. Don't congratulate yourself yet. Crying often doesn't really get going until babies are a few weeks old, then usually peaks at six weeks.

A crying baby is trying to tell you something. He may be trying to communicate that he's hungry or that he ate too much and his stomach hurts. He may be saying that his diaper is wet and it feels yucky or that he liked that nice, warm, wet diaper on him, and now that you took it off, he's cold—and mad! He may be saying that he's tired and wants you to rock him to sleep or that he's bored and wants you to samba dance for his entertainment. He may be saying that he's furious that he can't scoot across the carpet and grab the fireplace tools—in which case he's going to be crying for the next six or seven months (but will probably crawl early). When you first hold your baby in your arms, you won't understand any of this—and that's normal!

Your job is to figure out how to understand your infant's language, because crying is a language all its own. The sooner you figure it out, the sooner you'll spend more time listening to your baby coo and babble and less time listening to her shriek.

What you shouldn't be doing, at this point, is trying to teach your baby patience. In fact, the faster you respond to his cries, the better. It's easier to calm a baby that's just started crying, before it escalates into hysteria.

While no one has created a baby-cry/English dictionary, the pitch and rhythm of your baby's cry can provide a clue as to where to begin to look for the problem.

Mindful Mommy

A baby's cry makes both moms' and dads' heartbeats speed up, blood pressure increase, and palms sweat. It also heats up the breasts of nursing mothers; hearing your baby cry may soak your shirt with milk.

Reasons for Crying

Tired—A whimper or somewhat musical cry, it can be somewhat irregular, sometimes accompanied by eye or cheek rubbing. ("This one took us a while to figure out," said Cecily. "At first, we thought he fell asleep because he got so tired from crying. Then we realized that he was crying because he was tired.")

Sharp pain—A shriek, followed by a long silent pause and another shriek. (You'll definitely hear this one when your baby is vaccinated. It can also mean an air bubble is making her stomach hurt, that she has caught her foot in the bars of the crib, or she is being stabbed by a diaper pin.

Hunger—Short, rhythmic cries that can sound desperate.

Pooping—Starts out as more of a grunt than a cry, often while eating.

Too hot, sick, or feverish—A whiny cry.

Anger or frustration—Your baby may let out screams of outrage when you take a nipple from his mouth or unfasten his diaper, or for no apparent reason.

Boredom—Progresses from gurgling and grumbling to wailing. When you pick up a bored baby, the crying stops instantly.

Learn to Settle a Fussy Baby

Many of the same things that put your baby to sleep when she's tired will soothe her when she's fussy. For homemade white noise, turn on the bathroom fan, tune in static on the radio, or run the vacuum cleaner or dishwasher.

Doing laundry could kill two birds with one stone. If listening to the washer fill with water doesn't settle him down, sitting in his car seat near a vibrating dryer may. And you'll get something accomplished, too.

Don't be afraid to hand her over to someone else. If you're getting tired or frustrated, your baby will know it; a fresh pair of arms may solve the problem. If none are available, and you're reaching your limit, put her down in a safe place and take a short break.

Give yourselves a breath of fresh air—literally. Go outside and get some exercise. Go for a walk or ride a stationary bike with baby in a front pack. The motion may soothe your baby, and the exercise may soothe you. If the weather isn't cooperating, stay inside and dance, holding your baby close (music is optional).

Mommy Knows Best

A visit to a chiropractor may make some babies—particularly ones who had a rough birth—more comfortable and less tearful. Some mommies love this idea, some aren't comfortable with it, and studies don't consistently show it is better than placebo. It's up to you—do you have a chiropractor that you trust? Do you think it may help your baby?

More Soothing Options You Can Try

You've picked your baby up, offered to feed him, burped him, changed his diaper, wrapped him in a blanket, and taken the blanket off again—and he's still crying. You don't much care why anymore, and he may have forgotten why. You just want him to stop. It's time to try these all-purpose soothers.

Tried and True Soothers

Some soothing stuff you may want to add to your baby collection:

Sling—Sizes vary, depending on your height. You'll carry your baby more comfortably if you have the right size. Consider two slings, sized for mom and dad.

Aquarium—The sound of the filter is soothing, and the fish are distracting.

Swing—The tick-tick of a windup swing can be soothing, but this type needs to be rewound fairly often, and rewinding is loud. A battery-operated model may be a better choice. You won't use this for very many months, though, so borrow one if you can.

Sassy seat—A cloth-covered baby lounge chair that you can bounce with your feet.

Music—Try all kinds; if classical doesn't work, reggae might.

Front pack—a Snugli or Baby Bjorn will keep the baby close, and both your warmth and heartbeat may calm her.

Swaddling Can Help

In their first few weeks, some babies feel more secure, and are less likely to fuss, when wrapped snugly. Swaddling him will contain his flailing arms and legs, which may be startling him, and the heat from a dryer-warmed blanket will calm him down (other babies hate this and will quickly let you know). If your baby likes to be swaddled, see the figure below to learn how to do it.

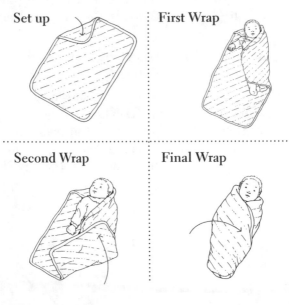

Set up

First Wrap

Second Wrap

Final Wrap

1. Position a square blanket like a diamond, and fold the top corner down.
2. Lay your baby on her back on the blanket, the top corner just above her neck. Tuck one arm down and fold the blanket around her body and behind her back.
3. Fold up the bottom part of the blanket, folding down any excess that would be covering her face.
4. Tuck the other arm down and fold the remaining corner of the blanket around her body and behind her back.

IDEAS FOR CALMING YOUR BABY

Keep it moving—Rock away in your glider or rocking chair in your nursery, or just rock back and forth wherever you are, sitting or standing. Dance slowly around the room. Walk him in the stroller—inside, outside, wherever.

Sing or chant—Soft, rhythmic coos may take your baby's mind off whatever is bothering her. You don't need to have a great voice or know the words, just hum something. If you really hate to sing, turn on the vacuum cleaner. It may not sound like much to you, but that annoying hum is music to some babies' ears.

Change the temperature—If you're not up for going outside, stand in front of the open fridge for a minute or two.

Change the scenery—Give your baby something interesting to look at. A plant, a mobile, or even a brightly patterned tablecloth will be interesting enough to distract him. Describe what you're looking at, and keep talking softly. He'll start to realize that he can't listen and scream at the same time.

Get naked—Babies like skin-to-skin contact—and dad's warm skin works just as well as mom's. Lay the baby down on your chest with your arms wrapped around her. Or, if she likes water, take a warm bath together.

Get quiet—Some babies may just need peace and quiet, together with no toys, no distractions. Leave him alone. Put him in a comfortable position in his crib or on a blanket on the floor, turn down the lights, and keep the noise down.

How You Can Minimize Crying

Babies are meant to be carried. In some cultures, babies are carried as much as 90 percent of the time, and they don't cry as much as babies in industrialized countries (who spend more of their time alone). In fact, researchers have confirmed that extra carrying results in dramatic reductions in crying. If you don't want your baby to let out more than an occasional whimper, don't put her down.

This isn't as onerous as it may seem. With such options as frontpacks and slings, and backpacks for older babies, your child can be "worn" comfortably for hours, leaving your hands free to do other things.

The Secret of the Sling

Once you figure out how to use it, a sling will be great for you and your baby. Your baby can hear your heartbeat, see your face, and catch a ride similar to what he felt in the womb. His weight is evenly distributed on your back, so you're comfortable, and both your hands are free to do what you want. The fact that he can sleep whenever he wants to, you can nurse discreetly, and you're touching him constantly is a benefit for you both.

Unlike putting a baby in a frontpack, which has a clear place for her head, arms, and legs to go, securing a baby in a sling is not intuitive. Your best bet is to get an experienced sling-wearer to show you. If that's not possible, refer to the illustration on page 32 for one method. (Note: Slings come in different sizes, based on the height of the wearer. Make sure yours fits.)

I discovered the power of the sling when I had my second child, Nadya. When she started to fuss, I would put her in her sling, go outside, fill my

Mommy Must

If you're going to use a sling, wash it many times before you first use it. The fabric will soften and it will be a lot more comfortable for you and for your baby.

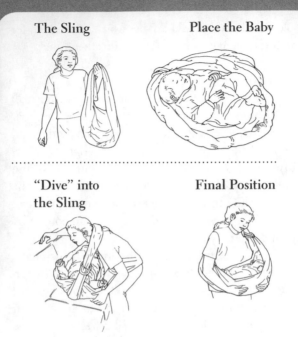

The Sling

Place the Baby

"Dive" into the Sling

Final Position

watering can, and water the plants on the back patio. By the time I had finished watering all the plants, she was usually asleep.

1. In your left hand, hold the sling by the ring, so the padded area, if there is one, is facing you, and the unpadded area is away from you.
2. Put the sling down on a couch, and smooth it out so that the ring is on the left end and the widest area is on the right. Open up the section that's on the bottom.
3. Place your baby on his back on the opened fabric so his head comes within a hand's width of

the ring and his feet are pointed toward the widest end.

4. Raise your right arm in the air, next to your ear, and dive into the sling with your arm and head. Adjust your position so the pad is on your left shoulder and the ring is near your left armpit.

5. Stand up, supporting your baby until you are sure he is secure.

Carrying Power

Here are some suggestions for holds that might calm or soothe your baby. Don't forget that for newborns, always support the head and bottom, and keep the baby as snuggled as possible—a baby that suddenly finds herself surrounded by not much more than air may startle.

NEWBORN HOLDS

Snuggle—Hold baby facing you, with his head resting on your chest, supporting his head and neck with one hand and his bottom with the other.

Football—Hold baby on one side of your body, supporting the head and neck with your hand and forearm.

Knee rest—With your legs together, put baby face up on thighs, head toward knees, baby's legs bent, holding your hands on either side of her body.

Shoulder—Supporting baby's head and neck, place him so that his head is resting on your shoulder. Support his bottom with your other arm.

Snuggle

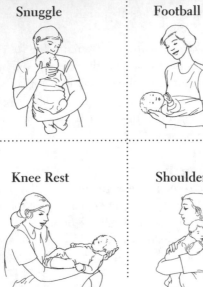

Football

Knee Rest

Shoulder

OLDER BABY HOLDS

Front Carry

Hip Carry

When It's Colic and What to Do

There are the cries that seem to have no rational cause and don't respond, at least for very long, to soothing. This may mean a baby is just venting at the end of a long day. But if the crying goes on for hours every day, at roughly the same time, several days a week, then you can feel justified in calling it colic. Some pediatricians use the Rule of Three to diagnose colic: crying for no apparent physical reason for three hours a day, three days a week, for three weeks. By this definition, one out of five babies has colic. In my case, it was two out of three. It wasn't until I had my third child that I discovered what it was like to have a baby that didn't scream for hours every day of his first three months. You get to finish your dinner, for one thing. You can sometimes talk to your spouse or watch TV—it's pretty amazing.

In spite of trying for more than fifty years, doctors haven't pinpointed the cause of colic. Historically, it is believed to be some kind of abdominal pain (the word "colic" is derived from *kolon*, which is Greek for "large intestine"), but even that's not certain.

Mindful Mommy

When your baby won't stop crying, place her in a front carrier and vacuum your house. The combination of the warmth of your body, the sound of the vacuum, and the rhythmic motion as you move back and forth across the floor is almost guaranteed to settle her down.

Colic may originate with an immature digestive system that operates with spasms instead of smooth muscle contractions. Or it may be that certain babies just notice the workings of their digestive system more. Some researchers have suggested that it may be an allergic reaction to something in the mother's diet—in particular, cow's milk. This theory is controversial, as colicky babies don't have any symptoms of the stomach problems associated with such an allergy, like diarrhea or vomiting. Colic may be the reaction of a baby worn out by trying to make sense of a busy day. Or, most likely, colic

Arm Drape

Colic Curl (forward)

Colic Curl (reverse)

Leg Pumping

may simply be the ordinary crying of a particularly strong willed and persistent baby.

What You Can Do

Since no one really knows what colic is, no one really knows how to fix it. You can try laying her face down, with her stomach over a small roll of towels or a warm hot-water bottle. There are several recommended colic positions:

Colic Remedies You Can Try

Motion—Rocking, riding in a stroller or a car, swinging in a baby swing (or even a car seat swung back and forth), dancing, bicycling his legs.

Medication—Simethicone is a nonprescription remedy that breaks down gas bubbles and is given to the baby in the form of drops. Brand names include Mylicon and Mylanta.

Teas—Make a tea of fennel, dill, caraway, anise, cumin, or coriander seeds by pouring one cup of boiling water over a teaspoon of seeds. Steep for fifteen minutes or less. Drink the tea yourself,

Mommy Must

Get help if you have a colicky baby. Incessant screaming can be overwhelming, so make sure you have some quiet time for yourself.

if you're nursing, or feed your baby a spoonful. Chamomile or mint tea is also an alternative.

Dietary changes—Try eliminating dairy products from your diet if you're nursing, or switch to a soy formula if you're bottle-feeding. The connection between cow's milk and colic is anecdotal at best, but some mothers have had success with this.

In spite of reports that all of these strategies work for some babies some of the time, odds are, if your baby is truly colicky, none of this will help much, and you'll just have to wait it out.

The point is to keep trying. And enlist your partner, your relatives, and your friends to help. Hold your baby, rock your baby, dance with your baby, or just sit and pat him—do anything that seems to help him calm down, even a little. It may seem pointless, but you will know you're trying, and maybe your baby will know, too.

The Fourth Month and Beyond

The good news is that parents of colicky babies should see the colic episodes begin to wind down significantly by the beginning of the fourth month (the Chinese consider a hundred days of crying to be normal). The bad news is that older babies can find new reasons for crying.

Chapter 4

Breastfeeding 101

UNLESS YOU OR YOUR baby has a condition that pre-cludes breastfeeding—please, please give it a try. If it doesn't work for you, you can phase-in bottles at any time. However, recent research indicates that women must breastfeed exclusively during the first three months in order for their milk supply to develop fully.

Milk from the Breast Is Best

For your baby's first six months of life, eating means milk—breastmilk or infant formula. More than 95 percent of mothers are physically capable of breast-feeding. If you can, you should.

Human milk is designed as the perfect food for infants. It contains elements that researchers are only beginning to discover. Over time, breastmilk changes from the colostrum produced in the first few days—which provides babies with antibodies to protect them from the germs they are encountering—to a blend of colostrum and milk, and eventually to pure milk.

Milk then adjusts in subtle ways as the baby matures; it even changes during the course of a feeding. A nursing baby first receives milk with a lower fat content; as he continues to feed, the fat content of the milk that follows increases. Breastmilk is powerful stuff. It can kill bacteria, viruses, intestinal parasites, and even stop the growth of cancer cells. Breast-fed babies develop fewer allergies and have a lower risk of developing diabetes.

Breastfeeding is easy. Most of you will discover this after the initial awkwardness. Others may find that the first few weeks of figuring out how to breastfeed correctly are a struggle. But hey, it took you at least that long to learn to ride a bicycle, and aren't you glad you did? In the long run, just like that bicycle, breastfeeding will make your life much easier. When your breast-fed baby is hungry, you pick her up, unsnap your nursing bra, and dinner is served. Once you get the hang of it, you'll probably manage to have a free hand—until it's time to unsnap the other side of your bra. You can read, dial a telephone, even shop for groceries (online or walking down store aisles) while your baby nurses in a sling.

Mommy Knows Best

Breastfed infants are less likely to be overweight when they reach first grade. According to a British study, children that were breastfed for more than a year were four times less likely to be overweight at school age than children who were breastfed for two months or less.

Breast size, unlike the medical conditions discussed later, is not a factor in breastfeeding success. Women with small breasts are not at a disadvantage. Instead, we may have an advantage—we can easily breastfeed with one hand, since we don't have to support the breast, just the baby. And we also may be encouraged to breastfeed longer by the thrill of, for once in our lives, being able to wear clothes that require cleavage.

When your bottle-fed baby is hungry, you have to check the refrigerator or the diaper bag and hope you find a prepared bottle, then warm it up while trying to distract your hungry and increasingly agitated baby. And bottle-feeding is a two-handed operation; you can't do much else while you're holding both the baby and the bottle. Breastmilk is easier to digest than formula, so breast-fed babies rarely get diarrhea or constipation and (trust me, this is a biggie) their dirty diapers don't stink. There is an odor, but not a particularly bad one. In fact, the stuff looks and kind of smells like Dijon mustard.

There are a host of other reasons to breastfeed— you may not get your period back for months and months, and you will probably look back on time spent breastfeeding as one of the most wonderful experiences of your life.

Doctor Recommended . . .

The American Academy of Pediatrics recommends that:

- Newborns nurse whenever they show signs of hunger

- Mothers breastfeed for at least the first twelve months of life and as long after as is mutually desired
- Babies breastfeed exclusively for the first six months of life
- No supplements—including water or formula—should be given to breastfeeding newborns unless there is a medical indication

... Mother Approved

In addition to the health and nutrition benefits of breastfeeding, there are the little perks of simplicity and cost savings. Breastfeeding babies are portable; you can take them anywhere for any amount of time without worrying about how long you can keep a bag of bottles cold or where you can find clean water to mix with powdered formula.

Breastfeeding is environmentally responsible—you don't have packaging, cans, or containers to throw out. You also don't have to worry about packing and lugging bottles, nipples, and paraphernalia with you, or trying to find what you need if you're away from home.

You will also reap the rewards of breastfeeding. It burns off fat better than a Stairmaster, and may protect you from breast cancer. Breastfeeding also mellows you out when you need it most; prolactin, the "mothering hormone," creates a feeling of calmness and well-being.

You May Need to Feed Your Baby Formula Part-or Full-Time If:

- You need to take a medication that would pass into your breastmilk and be dangerous to your baby (be sure to get clear information from your doctor)
- You return to work and do not have the opportunity to pump or are unable to pump enough milk
- You have had significant breast surgery. Often women with minor breast surgery, like the removal of benign lumps, have no problem breastfeeding. Breasts that were augmented also function fine, as long as the milk ducts were not cut.
- You have a highly contagious disease, like HIV or tuberculosis

The First Feeding

Your baby has just made his entrance into the world and, if he's doing fine, your partner or a nurse has placed him on your stomach. You can try to nurse him right away if you're up for it, but don't feel like you have to; waiting until you both get your bearings is fine. And even if you're ready, your baby may not be. Don't sweat it; there really is no rush. You'll both probably have a nap in the hours following the birth. Then you'll both wake up and be ready to tackle this new experience. And when you're in the hospital, there will be nurses, duolas, and even doctors that can help you and your baby for your first time!

On Your Mark

You'll probably want to start with the football hold or cradle hold (diagrammed on page 45-46). Sit up in bed, pull up your hospital gown, and settle a pillow on your lap. Make sure your back and elbows are supported; you may need more pillows. Get comfortable. If you have large breasts, tuck a rolled-up washcloth or towel under the breast you intend to nurse with to help support it. Then ask the nurse to hand you the baby.

Step by Step

Unwrap your baby and pull up her T-shirt, if she's wearing one—you want skin-on-skin contact. Rotate your baby to face your breast, supporting her head. Then, with the opposite hand, form a "C" with your thumb and forefinger and cup beneath your breast. Bring the baby close to your breast (don't lean down to the baby, that's a sure path to back pain), and lift up

Mommy Must

The first two weeks that you are breastfeeding are the hardest, and they don't give you a true picture of what it's really like. Stick with it through these challenging times before you even think about giving up. It will probably be worth it to you, in the end, to keep going!

your nipple, making sure not to cover the areola with your hand. Tickle the baby's lips with the tip of your nipple. Wait until she opens really wide and then, bringing her head to your breast, shove your breast in as far as it will go. If you weren't quick enough, your baby may have only the nipple in her mouth. Use your finger to break the suction, take her off the breast, and try again.

Once he's on, check his position. His mouth should be covering at least a third of the areola and you should hear sucks and swallows. Don't fuss about whether or not his nose seems to be covered by the breast—if he can't breathe, he'll move. Switch sides when you think your baby has drained the first breast; you won't hear swallowing anymore, or see his jaws or cheeks working. This may take as few as five minutes or as many as twenty or more. Take a burp break when you switch breasts.

Breastfeeding and Burping Positions

Cradle Hold

Cross-Cradle Hold
(opposite arm)

Football Hold

Side-lying Hold

Double Football (twins)

Shoulder (high over shoulder)

Lap (sitting upright)

Knees (tummy down)

Get Set

Nurse your baby on both breasts, and do so at least eight times a day for at least the first week. Don't worry if you don't seem to have any milk yet; it will take a few days for your milk to come in. Frequent nursing at this point is intended to establish a good milk supply. Full-term babies can go without anything to eat or drink for days, giving you both plenty of time to learn how to breastfeed. You may have to remind the nurses of this when they suggest giving him a bottle of water or formula.

At the first feeding, and over the next few days, your baby will be receiving the yellowish fluid called colostrum. Colostrum is full of antibodies and will protect your baby from a host of viruses and infections. It also acts as a laxative that flushes out the meconium—the black, tarry waste accumulated before birth.

Your baby's feeding during these early nursing sessions will trigger the release of prolactin, which relaxes you and stimulates milk production. It will also release another hormone, oxytocin. Oxytocin causes muscle contractions in the milk lobes, which

Mindful Mommy

Make sure you're comfortable before breastfeeding. Find a comfy spot and get lots of pillows, a big drink of water, milk, or watered-down juice, and a book or the TV remote. Put the portable phone within reach or turn the answering machine on.

will force the milk down into the milk ducts, and in the uterus, which will speed your postpartum recovery.

Keeping It Simple

Breastfeeding is natural, rewarding, and good for both you and your baby. However, it is not always easy. While you're both still learning, there are several things you can do to keep things going smoothly:

- Get comfortable.
- Bring the baby to you, instead of moving yourself to the baby.
- Make sure the baby is latched on correctly. She should have the areola in her mouth, not just the nipple. If it hurts, it's wrong.
- Make sure your baby's head is tipped slightly back and his chin is pressed into your breast. It is the movements of his chin and tongue that draw out the milk.
- Keep your wrist straight. Flexing the wrist that is supporting your baby's head may tip her down into a less efficient nursing position, and the strain on your wrist may cause inflammation and pain.
- Nurse at least ten to twelve times a day for the first few weeks—that's an average of every two hours.
- Don't watch the clock; let your baby tell you when he's done.

- Have a drink. When your baby is drinking, you should be, too—water.
- Vary your nursing position. The baby will press on your breasts differently depending on how she is positioned.
- Use your finger to break the suction before taking your baby off your nipple. Pulling him off will hurt.

Don't forget to burp your baby. Most babies swallow a little air along with the milk, and this trapped air can cause stomach pains. Try burping when you switch sides and after you're finished. But don't worry if your baby doesn't burp; some just don't.

Checking in with the Doctor

If you're feeling insecure or aren't sure if the baby is sucking correctly or you feel uncomfortable in any way, get some expert advice. If you're in the hospital, buzz for the nurse (if you're at home, your midwife will probably still be with you) and ask her to call the lactation consultant, if she's available. If not, ask the nurse to help you position yourself and the baby.

Breastfeeding Styles

As with sleeping and crying habits, babies' feeding styles vary from baby to baby, as well as individually, depending on what the baby needs at the time. You may notice your baby prefers one of the following styles. (The first five names were coined by researchers at Yale University.)

Barracuda: Immediately latches on and feeds vigorously for ten to twenty minutes.

Excited Ineffective: Goes wild at the sight of the breast, grabs it, loses it, and then screams. Try to feed this baby before she's too hungry, and consider getting help with your latch-on technique.

Procrastinator: This baby will wait for the real milk, thank you very much, and he'll pass on the colostrum. Don't let this initial lack of interest trick you into giving him a bottle of water or formula; just keep trying to latch him on at regular intervals. Pump between feedings to ensure a sufficient milk supply.

Gourmet: This baby will take a delicate taste of the milk, roll it around in her mouth, and perhaps play with the nipple a little before getting down to business. She doesn't like to be rushed.

Rester: This baby likes to nurse a few minutes, rest a few minutes, nurse a few minutes more, take a nap, and then come back for more. Make sure you find a comfortable seat and surround yourself with books, snacks, or whatever you need to keep you happy for what can be a long feeding session.

Billy Goat: This baby butts, tugs, and pummels you while he feeds. He may be frustrated with your milk flow, which may be too slow or too fast for his taste.

Regurgitator: This baby nurses contently for about twenty minutes, then throws half of it back up on your shirt. Then, of course, she's hungry again.

Barnacle: This baby latches on tightly and nurses constantly, almost around the clock.

Sightseer: This baby doesn't want to miss the passing scene, so his eyes and head wander about while he's nursing. If you have a sightseer, you'll be surprised by just how far your nipples can stretch. Sightseeing tends to emerge in the fourth or fifth month.

Desserter: About twenty minutes after a full nursing session, this baby comes back for a couple more sips—for dessert.

What's in a Name?

Think about what you are going to name the act of breastfeeding because, sooner than you think, your baby will be using that word. Some common names: "boobie," "the boob," "ba," "snack," "lunch," "nurse," "nurch," "drink," "dahda," "mimi," "mother's milk," and "bup." Some babies have made their own choices—one of my friend's toddlers shouts "Feed you!" when she wants to nurse; another says "Off, please." (At least she's polite.)

Go!

When your milk comes in—two to four days after birth—replacing the colostrum, you will know it. Your normally squishy breasts will get bigger than you ever imagined possible and may seem as hard as

51

rocks. This won't last; you may want to put on your skimpiest bathing suit and take a picture, because otherwise you'll never believe you were ever this big.

Fetch your baby and start nursing, because the longer you wait, the more your breasts will hurt. If your breasts are too hard for your baby to latch on to, put a warm washcloth on them for a few minutes or take a shower. You can also massage your milk glands toward your nipple and squeeze out a little milk.

For some women, this transition from colostrum to milk can be rough, but at least it doesn't last long—typically just a day.

Now when your baby begins to feed, you may feel a tingling or burning sensation a moment before milk begins to leak from your breasts. This is the let-down reflex, caused by the release of oxytocin, which triggers contractions in the muscles surrounding the milk-producing cells to squeeze the milk into the milk ducts. You don't need to be feeding a baby to trigger this reflex. It can happen during sex, when you see a picture of a baby—the TV commercial for Pampers always used to get me going—if you hear a baby cry, and sometimes for no

Mommy Knows Best

If you are still uncomfortable after your baby nurses, put ice on your breasts for a few minutes or tuck a cold cabbage leaf into your bra—seriously! Cabbage, possibly because of its sulfur content, draws out the excess fluid to reduce swelling, and the cold feels good.

apparent reason. If you don't feel it, you'll still know milk is flowing because your baby will start gulping. She may also pull away for a moment if the milk is spraying too fast.

Handy Accessories

The nice thing about breastfeeding is you really don't need anything but your baby and your body. But it's nice to have:

- Lots of pillows to tuck around you.
- A nursing pillow. There are several types: a wedge that sits on your lap; a wide, partial ring for your waist (great for football holds or nursing twins); and the Brest Friend, which is a smaller ring with a back support.
- A nursing stool. This is a low stool that lifts your legs just enough to ease the strain on your lower back.
- Cloth diapers. Lots of them—to catch messy burps and drool.
- Snap-front nursing bras. They are easier to manage one-handed than those with hooks.
- An electric pump. The popular Medela Pump-in-Style is usually powerful enough; if you need all the power you can get, rent a hospital-grade pump.
- A nursing dress. You will eventually get sick of untucked shirts, so one official nursing dress is nice to have.
- A sling. Great for nursing while on the run.

- Paperback books. Nursing is a great time to catch up on your reading, but magazines or hardcover books are hard to manage.

How to Maintain Your Milk Supply

You will be best able to breastfeed successfully—barring one of the medical situations previously discussed—if you get plenty of rest, surrender to your baby, and are surrounded by people who support you. If friends or relatives are uncomfortable at the sight of you breastfeeding, or keep questioning your ability to feed your baby, avoid them. If your baby wants to nurse every hour or two, let him. His stomach will eventually get bigger. He'll become strong enough to feed more efficiently, and time between feedings will increase.

Concerned about Your Milk Supply?

Take more naps, make sure you are eating and drinking enough (a dehydrating airplane trip once destroyed my milk supply for about a day and a half), and let your baby feed more frequently (if she's using a pacifier, you might want to take it away for a while).

Mommy Must

Teas made of thistle or borage leaves or fennel seeds have been reported to boost your milk production, as has oatmeal. Eat a bowl in the late afternoon for a boost in the evening, when your milk supply is likely to be at its lowest.

Moms report success with a number of natural supplements that seem to increase milk production. These may or may not work for you, but it probably won't hurt to try one or more.

Perhaps one of the oldest and most common prescriptions for boosting milk production is a glass of beer every evening. Alcohol metabolizes quickly in adults, and therefore one glass is unlikely to affect the baby. But again, don't overdo it. It seemed to work for me. When we were both nursing, my friend Jodi and I would occasionally split a bottle of beer at 5 P.M. I don't know whether it worked because of the extra fluid, the hops, the tranquilizing effect of alcohol, or the fact that we both sat and yakked for an hour or so while we were drinking it.

What about Bottles?

At some point, be it soon after the baby's birth or some time later—say, when your favorite musician is on tour and you really, really want to go to a four-hour concert without worrying about what the loud music is doing to your baby's ears—it may occur to you that it would be nice if your infant had a friendly acquaintance with a bottle. You decide to introduce them.

If you think you'll ever want your baby to take a bottle, get him used to it when he is between four and six weeks old. Too soon could affect your milk supply unless you pump regularly; too much later and he might not cooperate.

Side Effects: Leaking and More

Leaking is most common in the early weeks of nursing, but can happen at any time, particularly when you're used to nursing your baby at fairly regular intervals but get delayed. Leaking can also be triggered by the sound or sight of a baby—any baby—or by sex. My friend Amy even leaked when she heard a dog whine. While leaking itself isn't a problem, the round wet spot on your shirt can be. To avoid or minimize this, wear print shirts, use breast pads or a thick cotton bra, and press against your breasts with your forearm when you begin to feel the tingle that signals a let-down.

Ouch! Sore Nipples

Sore nipples are typically caused by incorrect positioning or improper latch-on. To get over a case of sore nipples, first, solve the positioning problem. Then you can:

- Air-dry your nipples after every nursing. You can also make sure your nipples get air by cutting the handles off of two tea strainers (preferably plastic) and placing them over your nipples, inside your bra.
- Catch some rays. Find a discreet sunny spot, or use a sun lamp, and sun for three minutes several times a day.
- Express a little breastmilk and dab it on your nipples. Breastmilk has a number of healing properties—take advantage of them.

- Make a cup of tea, then save the tea bag. Used tea bags also have healing properties. Place one (at room temperature) on your sore nipple for a few minutes.
- Soothe them with a lotion. Lanolin is often recommended, but it can contain pesticide residues. Olive oil or gel from an aloe vera leaf (wash your nipple before nursing) are alternatives.
- Apply ice before nursing. Ice acts as a painkiller and helps bring out your nipples for a better latch-on.
- Take a break. Spend a day nursing on only one side to give the other nipple a chance to recover. Either hand express or pump the resting breast as often as you would nurse.

You can also use nipple shields, but do so only as a last resort. These silicon shells fit over your nipples and cushion them while the baby sucks milk through them. If you do use them, take them off halfway through the feeding.

Your Baby's Breastfeeding Quirks

All babies are different, especially when it comes to breastfeeding. As you and your baby both get used to nursing, you will get to know your baby's breastfeeding preferences and habits.

Breast Favoritism

Most babies will prefer one breast to the other. It may be because of the way you support the baby with your stronger arm, the fact that one breast produces more milk, or that the baby simply prefers to lie on one side instead of the other. To avoid having the less-desired breast go completely into retirement (and make you look lopsided for the duration of breastfeeding), start each feeding with the breast that is out of favor. Your baby may be less likely to be picky when she's really hungry.

Rejection

You can feel pretty insulted when your baby pulls off and cries after nursing for a few minutes and refuses to latch on again. The key to ending rejection is finding the cause. Most common? A flood of milk—too much for your baby to handle. If you suspect that this is the problem, express or pump a little milk before you nurse your baby. If that doesn't fix it, your baby may have a cold or earache, be teething, hate your new deodorant, or have found that something you ate changed the taste of the milk. It may be as simple as the weather—on a hot day your baby may not want to snuggle against your warm body— or a developmental spurt—your baby suddenly has noticed the world around him. If you can't figure out the cause, hang in there; hunger will eventually prevail.

Biting

Many breastfeeding moms get bitten at least once when the first teeth come in. They typically let out a yell, startle their baby into tears, then feel horrible about scaring their baby. The baby, however, doesn't try that again for quite a while. If you have a biter, use your finger to take the baby off of your breast, say "No" distinctly and calmly, and hold her off a few seconds before letting her suck again. This usually works after a few bites.

Breastfeeding Hurdles

Most speed bumps you encounter as you nurse can be diagnosed and treated at home and can be prevented with a little extra self-care.

Clogged Milk Duct

A clogged milk duct is fairly obvious—you feel a small lump in your breast, and it can be painful. (The lump can be anywhere in the ducts, which run all over.) To treat it, put a warm washcloth over it for five minutes, then massage the lump gently, pushing the milk down toward your nipple. Then start nursing your baby, making sure the baby is positioned so he faces the clogged duct, and continue massaging. The more you nurse, the faster the clogged duct will drain.

Breast Infections (Mastitis)

Breast infections are serious. If you have flu-like symptoms, a low fever, red streaks or patches on the breast skin, pain in your breast, or a hard lump in your breast, you may have one. Go to bed, drink lots of fluid, apply warm compresses, and continue to nurse on both sides. If you're not better the next morning, call your healthcare provider for an antibiotic.

Absolutely do not stop nursing; that will only make the infection worse. Do not delay treatment of a breast infection. Untreated infections can abscess and require surgery. While some mothers may think about trying to cure mastitis without antibiotics—don't. It is not worth getting an abscess, and the antibiotics won't hurt your breastfeeding baby. If you want to use natural remedies, go ahead, but take your antibiotics as well.

Thrush

Also called a yeast infection, true thrush isn't that common. In fact, thrush today is a popular catch-all diagnosis for any kind of nipple pain. You may simply have a baby who is a strong feeder and hurts you for a few seconds until she latches on correctly. If you actually do have thrush, you will have cracked nipples that burn the entire time your baby nurses. To control thrush, make sure your nipples and everything that touches them are clean, use a nipple wash (a teaspoon of vinegar in one cup of water), or nystatin cream (a prescription drug) that stops yeast from reproducing.

Common Drugs: Are They Safe for the Baby?	
YES:	NO:
Acetaminophen	Tetracycline
Antihistamines (maybe, check with your doctor)	Cyclosporine
Ibuprofen	Anticancer drugs
Robitussin (guaifenesin)	Amphetamines
Antidepressants	Nicotine
Decongestants	
Most antibiotics	
Antacids	
Thyroid medications	
Insulin	
Kaopectate	
Vitamins	
Vaccines	

No Let-Down Reflex

Some women have trouble breastfeeding at first because they aren't experiencing a let-down. In fact, some women who give up breastfeeding because

Mommy Knows Best

Stress is the biggest inhibitor of the let-down reflex, so anything that can reduce stress helps, like a warm bath or listening to music.

they think they don't have enough milk actually have plenty of milk; they just don't have a let-down reflex. Without the let-down reflex, the baby gets a trickle of milk—enough to sip, but not to gulp.

There are also prescription medications that might jumpstart a let-down, including Reglan, a prescription anti-nausea drug that can increase milk supply. I took Reglan briefly after a drug I was given for a migraine headache trashed my milk supply; nursing was quickly brought back on track. Reglan, however, should not be taken by anyone with a history of depression.

Milk Overflow

Milk coming too fast may make your baby gulp, choke, or pull away. You may want to express a little milk first. Try nursing from just one breast at each feeding; you may have to pump the other one in between feedings if you're uncomfortable. Try leaning back in a recliner or on pillows while nursing, positioning your baby so the top of her head is above the top of your breast, so she can "sip" at the milk without it pouring down her throat.

Flat or Inverted Nipples

If your nipples don't protrude when you're aroused—or in a cold breeze—you may have what the breastfeeding books define as inverted nipples. To check, squeeze the areola at the bottom of the nipple and press it toward your chest. If your nipple doesn't protrude, it is flat. Truly inverted nipples can prevent successful breastfeeding, but most will respond to treatment—manually rolling your nipples several times a day, wearing a cup inside your bra that presses the areola and encourages the nipple to protrude, or pumping with a heavy-duty pump.

Call a Doctor If . . .
- Your baby hasn't had a wet diaper in twelve to twenty-four hours
- It is the fourth day after the birth and you see no evidence of white-colored milk in leakage from your breast or spit from the baby
- Your baby has no bowel movements on the fourth day after the birth
- Your baby cannot latch on to a breast
- Your baby is lethargic and is difficult to wake for feedings
- Your baby latches on readily, but feeds for only a minute or two and then appears to doze off
- Your baby feeds endlessly, for an hour at a time, and doesn't seem satisfied, then sleeps for less than an hour before crying for another feeding
- Your breasts are painfully hard and swollen; full and firm is fine, hot and painful is not
- Your nipples hurt during the entire feeding, not just for a moment at latch-on, and you find yourself dreading feedings or shortening them because of the pain

Dress for Success

While special nursing clothes are available, you don't really need them. You can't wear regular dresses and breastfeed easily, but any untucked shirt is fine for nursing (and can often let you nurse more discretely than special shirts with slits). A nursing bra is good for easy access. Avoid tight bras or underwire bras; they can cause clogged milk ducts.

You'll probably want at least a small supply of breast pads to catch leaks in the early weeks, and then for any time you think you'll be away from your baby for longer than usual. I usually needed a breast pad while I was nursing to catch the let-down from the opposite breast. Change the pads regularly to keep your breasts dry. Disposable pads lined with plastic block air; washable cotton breast pads are better. Whatever you choose to wear, during the first few weeks, you'll be struggling to figure out how to breastfeed and feeling as if all you do all day is feed your baby. This is not the time to decide how long you'll breastfeed. Just get going without a stop date in mind. Months will pass. You may add bottles—of breast milk or formula—into the routine when you

Mindful Mommy

You can make your own breast pads as an alternative to disposable pads and premade cotton pads. To make your own, fold up a cloth handkerchief or cut circles from cotton diapers or old T-shirts (you'll need several layers).

go back to work or need some time to yourself. By the age of six months, your baby will probably start eating cereal and other mushy foods, and you'll be nursing even less.

The current recommendation of the AAP is to breastfeed throughout the first year of your baby's life, and then as long as is mutually desirable. Your baby may wean himself before then—or not. You may want to continue breastfeeding into the second year—or not. You may wean to a bottle or find that your baby does just fine with a cup. You may decide to wean because you are pregnant with another child, or choose to continue breastfeeding through your next pregnancy. Once you've made a successful start at breastfeeding, the options for continuing are all yours.

Chapter 5

Bottle Basics You Should Know

UNLIKE BREASTS (YOU'VE GOT one pair, and your baby is pretty sure to accept their shape and what comes out of them), bottle-feeding presents you with a number of somewhat confusing options. Whether it's equipment or formulas, prepare yourself for a trial (and error) period as you figure out what you and your baby like best.

Guilt-Free Bottle-Feeding

It used to be that nursing mothers were banished to a bathroom stall, worried about the negative attention they'd attract if they breastfed in public. Now, bottle-feeders are being pushed into the closet.

If you've made the decision to bottle-feed, don't second-guess yourself. There is no going back, so smile at the people who may glare at you and explain if you'd like, but don't beat yourself up about it. Your child will give you plenty of other things to stew about, so save your energy.

Choosing Your Equipment

First, there is the bottle. The three types of bottles (glass, plain plastic, and plastic with disposable liners) come in two sizes: small (four ounces) or large (eight or nine ounces).

That's where simplicity ends. Since each manufacturer tries to distinguish itself from the others, there are hordes of variations within each category. You will find short, fat bottles and long, thin ones. There are ones with a bend in the middle and ones with handles.

The general idea behind all these bottle designs is to make it harder for air to get into the baby. Bottles with liners collapse as the baby sucks. The ones with the bend are intended to be easier to hold at just the right air-bubble-preventing angle, but they're harder to clean. Except for your convenience and your baby's preference, the bottle you choose doesn't matter all that much.

Mommy Must

Buy more bottles and nipples than you think you'll need. If you don't have enough, you'll end up scrubbing bottles all day!

Nipples

What does matter is nipple choice. Nipples differ in size, shape, and flexibility. You want a nipple that most resembles the human breast. If you're bottle-feeding from the beginning, your options are open—a generic "breast" nipple is fine; but if you are transitioning to bottle-feeding from breastfeeding, you need to be more selective. The nipple's shape should resemble yours. For example, if you have large breasts with fairly flat nipples, your baby may be uncomfortable drinking from a long nipple on a small base. You may need to let your baby test a couple of shapes before you discover what works best. There are a lot more varieties available than those on the grocery store shelf; ask your doctor or check the web.

Standard

Orthodontic

Wide-based

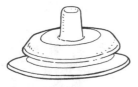

Wide Transition

When you're shopping for a nipple, you'll notice brownish nipples and clear nipples. The brown nipples are typically made of latex; the clear ones are silicon. If you can find a silicon nipple in the size and shape you need, I'd recommend it over the rubber one, which has a more noticeable flavor and gets sticky when it gets old. Because the rubber ones are opaque, it's also harder to be sure they're clean.

The other key variable is the hole in the nipple. Some nipples have multiple holes, some have one. Some holes are small, some large. Some are round pricks, and some are cut in an X shape. According to the manufacturers' labels, the small, slow-flow holes are for newborns, while larger, faster-flow nipples are intended for older babies. But the manufacturer doesn't always know best, and your baby may have a different idea.

Because I had a strong let-down, my kids were used to gulping milk, and slow-flowing infant nipples made them scream in frustration. I finally tried opening up the hole in one nipple with a hot needle so that the milk nearly poured out. When that modification turned my baby into a reasonably willing bottle-feeder, I replaced the newborn nipples with the fastest-flowing nipples I could find.

Mommy Knows Best

For a faster milk flow, loosen the neck ring. If that doesn't help, you can enlarge the hole of a latex nipple with a needle heated in a flame, or boil the nipple for a few minutes with a toothpick stuck through the hole.

Even if you have the right nipple, you may not always get the right flow of milk, or even the same flow you got the last time. Turn the bottle upside down and shake it a few times. You should see a spritz of milk followed by slow, steady drops. You can adjust the flow by loosening or tightening the bottle's ring. You may also find that some supposedly fast-flowing nipples are slower than those advertised as slow-flowing—check the flow rates for yourself. Be aware that nipple flow may change (typically, but not always, slowing down) with repeated washings.

Additional Paraphernalia

After you choose your bottles and nipples, you'll find that you'll need a few more gadgets to simplify preparing, cleaning, and traveling. The good news is that you won't need everything on this list. The better news is that most of the items will be useful long after your baby is beyond bottles.

- Bottles—if you're bottle-feeding exclusively, you'll need eight four-ounce bottles for a newborn and eight eight-ounce bottles for an older baby
- A bottle brush
- A graduated pitcher for mixing batches of formula
- A basket designed to hold rings and nipples for the dishwasher (you'll use it later for all sorts of things)

- Bottle warmers—these pads heat up when activated by pinching, and can be recharged by boiling
- Formula dispenser for traveling—a plastic case with several compartments for premeasured powdered formula; a two-chambered bottle—one chamber holds powdered formula, one holds water; or premeasure formula into bottle liners, twist-tie shut, and mix with premeasured water kept in a separate bottle

So What Goes in the Bottle?

Next is the question of what goes in the bottle. If you're pumping and have a supply of breastmilk, you're all set. If not, you need to select a formula. There are milk-based and soy-based formulas. According to recent research, soy-based formulas do not lower the risk of allergies or colic, and may have problems of their own. There are also formulas that are specially processed to break down the milk proteins, which makes them easier to digest and less likely to cause allergies. These "protein hydrolysate formulas" taste terrible and cost twice as much as standard formulas, but can be a boon for some babies.

You may have to try various formulas if your baby seems to reject one, vomits after most feedings, has constant diarrhea, or gets a rough red rash on the face or bottom (no two are exactly alike, so taste test them yourself). Any formula you use should be iron fortified. Low-iron formulas, which were once thought to prevent colic and constipation, are not nutritionally complete. Some organizations are now lobbying for them to be taken off the market. Any standard formula is fine, as long as your baby likes it and seems to digest it well.

Formulas come packaged as a powder, concentrated liquid, or ready-to-serve liquid. Powder is the cheapest, most compact, and most portable, but is slightly more difficult to blend than the concentrated liquid.

Fill 'Er Up

You'll want to boil the nipples and other bottle parts before the first use—this sterilizes them and gets rid of the plastic flavor. After that, for a healthy, full-term infant, you don't really have to sterilize them again, as long as you have a chlorinated water supply; well water can be a concern. Have your water tested for safety or put the bottles in a pot and boil them for five minutes prior to each use. I know your mother spent hours sterilizing your bottles. Guess what? She did all that work for nothing. For all subsequent washings, a run through the dishwasher or

Mindful Mommy

Take an educated guess at how many bottles your baby will need during a day and make them in one batch, in the morning, when your baby isn't screaming with hunger.

hand washing in hot, soapy water will get them sufficiently clean. You'll find that it's best to wash or soak bottles soon after using—curdled milk can be difficult to scrub out.

Next, wash your hands, wipe off the top of the formula can, and mix the formula exactly according to the directions (unless you're using a ready-to-use formula, of course). Too little water can cause dehydration and too much water means your baby won't be getting enough calories.

Pour the formula into the bottle. You probably think the next thing you need to do is to warm the bottle and then shake a few drops on your wrist to check the temperature, just like you've seen on TV. Wrong. In fact, unless your baby is used to a warm bottle, he probably won't care if you serve it to him at room temperature or straight out of the refrigerator, although he may get used to (and come to prefer) the bottle temperature he gets most often. Think of the advantages of a baby that will drink a cold bottle: There's no struggling to warm a bottle while holding a hungry, crying, and increasingly agitated baby and no looking for hot water while on a trip. You can put

Mommy Knows Best

If you are concerned about the amount of chlorine in your tap water, use bottled water. It isn't necessary to boil the water unless the available water supply has known problems.

a bottle in a cooler of ice right next to your bed for nighttime feedings.

If your gourmet child insists on warm bottles, go ahead and do that little wrist ritual—if the milk feels at all hot, it is too hot. If you've microwaved the milk in the bottle to heat it, shake it well, so there are no hot spots. Keep in mind that you should not microwave breastmilk, at any cost—put it in a cup of warm water if you want to warm it.

10 Bottle-Feeding Mistakes

1. Boiling bottles to sterilize them is not really necessary. A trip through the dishwasher or a soap-and-hot-water wash is sufficient.
2. Don't change the proportion of water to formula (either because you think it's a hot day, so your baby needs more water, or that extra formula will make him sleep better). You risk dehydrating or starving your baby.
3. Don't boil water to mix with powdered formula. Unless your water supply has known problems (in which case you may wish to use bottled water), water straight from the tap or filter is fine.
4. Don't leave the top on the bottle while heating in the microwave.
5. Don't microwave breastmilk (it destroys valuable nutrients).
6. Don't forget to shake bottles that contain microwaved milk to eliminate hot spots.

7. Don't give your baby a bottle to hold in the crib. This can cause tooth decay and ear infections.
8. Be careful not to screw the nipple ring down too tightly. This cuts off the flow of milk and makes bottle-feeding frustrating for the baby.
9. Babies too young to hold a bottle should not be allowed to drink without someone holding them. Propping a bottle to let a baby feed herself can cause choking.
10. Don't urge your baby to finish a bottle. Breast-fed babies eat until they are full; bottle-fed babies should be allowed the same privilege.

When Dinner Is Served

Settle into a comfortable chair with a nearby table on which to rest the bottle when you stop to reposition the baby. Turn off the phone and try to minimize other distractions. Hold your baby snuggled close, positioning his head in line with the rest of his body. He should be at about a 45° angle, so that his ears are higher than his mouth and his head tips back slightly. If your baby spits up during the feeding, adjust the angle, but don't hold your baby completely flat; the milk can back up into the Eustachian tube and cause an ear infection.

Pick up the bottle and then, with one finger on the hand holding the bottle, stroke the baby's cheek that is closest to your body. When he turns toward you, brush his lips with the nipple and let him latch on himself; don't stuff it in. Make sure the tip of the nipple is in the back of his mouth. Hold the bottle firmly so it resists his suction; otherwise, he'll just be moving the bottle around, instead of getting the milk out.

As she drinks, keep adjusting the angle of the bottle so that the nipple is always full of milk, not air. Don't tip the bottle up any more than you have to; the more you tip it up, the faster the flow, and a gulping baby is likely to swallow air. If the flow is too slow, however, your baby may get frustrated and fuss or lose interest and doze off.

When your baby seems to fuss or pull away, stop for a burp, then offer him the bottle again. If he's not interested, don't push him to finish the bottle. And don't obsess about how much your baby eats; nursing mothers don't know how much their babies get, and breastfed babies do just fine. The amounts will vary from day to day, so just make sure that your baby is steadily gaining weight.

Mindful Mommy

If your baby doesn't finish a bottle of breast milk, you don't have to throw out the leftovers. Put it back in the refrigerator and bring it out for the next feeding; but to be safe, don't do this more than twice. Leftover formula breeds bacteria more easily than breastmilk, so unfinished amounts should be thrown away.

When to Bring on the Bottle

If you're breastfeeding and intend to occasionally use a bottle or eventually switch to a bottle full-time, timing is everything. The best time to introduce a bottle is after the third week and before the eighth week. If you start too early, you may permanently reduce your milk supply; if you start too late, your baby may not want to have anything to do with a bottle. After the third week, conduct bottle practice every day. Once your baby has demonstrated that she is willing and able to suck from a bottle's nipple, you don't have to continue with daily bottles, but do remind her at least several times a week that milk does, indeed, come in bottles. Be prepared, though: At six or eight months, she may pull a fast one on you and begin refusing bottles no matter how successful she's been with them until that point.

Another Chance

If you miss this bottle introduction window, your baby may want nothing to do with a bottle, and it may not be worth forcing the issue. You can just wait another month or two and then begin teaching your baby to drink from a cup. But if you must wean an unwilling baby to a bottle (because you have to be away from your baby or must take medication that would be dangerous for your baby, for example), it can be done.

First, make sure that you are holding the baby in a different position than the one in which you breastfeed—facing out, for example—or feed while walking around the room. When you are getting ready to give your baby the bottle, act thrilled and excited, as if you are just about to give him a delightful treat; don't act apologetic or worried. Expect your baby to reject your first attempts. Give up for a few moments, then try again, still acting as enthusiastic as you possibly can. Remember that even a few swallows taken from a bottle count as a win.

You can start by offering the bottle a few times a day when the baby is hungry, but if she refuses, take it away. You might try offering a cup or waiting a little while and then nursing her. If that doesn't work, try completely skipping a feeding, then offer a bottle at the next feeding. The opposite method may work for some babies. That is, introduce the bottle when the baby is not frantically hungry, in hopes that it will be perceived as something fun to play with, and then—what a bonus—the baby gets some milk, too. If this doesn't work, temporarily switch to a dropper or syringe; try anything that will get the milk into the baby's mouth from a source other than the breast.

If you're the nursing mother and are having no success with bottle-feeding, get yourself out of the picture. Let someone else struggle with this early introduction. Typically, most moms turn to the dads, but even better is an experienced bottle-feeder—her confidence will communicate to the baby.

Pumping 101

Did you ever see a milking machine demonstration at a county fair? Try to picture yourself in the cow's place. "No way!" you think.

That's what I thought when I had my first baby, anyway. No way am I hooking myself up to one of those electric milking machines. So when my son Alexander was born, I bought a small and much more friendly looking hand pump. I pumped for a frustrating half-hour a day for weeks, squeezing out a few drops of milk each time, trying to fill a bottle so my husband and I could go out alone for our upcoming anniversary. I did everything I was supposed to: I picked a comfortable chair, used a warm compress, and looked at a picture of Alexander, but still only got a few drops. I got a few more when I tried to pump and nurse Alexander simultaneously, but it was a struggle to do that without dropping him. I eventually gave up and used formula for relief bottles, and then wished I hadn't. The more formula he drank, the less milk I produced, and the more formula he wanted.

When I had my daughter Nadya, I got over my milking machine phobia and rented a heavy-duty double-barreled electric breast pump, and was able to get three to four ounces in seven minutes every day while I watched Oprah. (The bad news was that I started getting a let-down every time Oprah came on.) I pumped every day, and soon had a freezer full of breastmilk. In spite of this abundant supply, Nadya never did take to a bottle. So she had breastmilk in her sippy cup and on her cereal until she was about a year old. (I even tried it in my coffee one day, having run out of regular milk. If you're ever tempted to do that—don't.)

I pumped again with my third child, Mischa, wondering if I should bother, given that he wasn't really impressed with bottles, either. Then one day, when he was less than three months old, I was flattened by a migraine headache. The emergency room doctor gave me a shot for the pain, reassuring me that the medication was safe for a breastfeeding baby. Safe, maybe; however, the drug was an antihistamine that trashed my milk supply. Over the next three days, my husband used up every bag of milk stored in the freezer, while I lay on the couch.

Why Bother Pumping?

Having a supply of pumped breastmilk on hand may be a good idea. Even if you rarely give your baby a bottle, at least she will recognize what's inside of it. However, if you don't have a reason to pump—for instance, no plan to go back to work or to attend an event to which you can't bring your baby—and you

Mommy Must

If you do decide to pump, get the most powerful pump you can. Some women with hair-trigger let-downs can use a hand pump or even express milk without a pump, but you'll have a better chance of success with a hospital-grade pump. Portable briefcase-style electric pumps aren't bad, but are not quite as strong as the less stylish ones.

don't want to, then don't. Just plan on bringing your baby with you whenever you go out for more than a few hours until she's eating solids. (It's only six months.)

Finding a Rhythm

Wait until your baby is at least four weeks old and, hopefully, settled into a regular nursing schedule. Pick a time at least an hour after he's nursed and an hour before you expect him to nurse again (or a time when there is something on TV that you like, since it's hard to pump and do much else but sit), and try to pump at the same time every day. If your baby for some reason cuts a feeding short, pump out the remainder. If you experience a let-down during a free moment, grab the pump and take advantage of it.

Use clean pump equipment and bottles (wash with hot soapy water and air dry on a clean towel or run through the dishwasher). Wash your hands, get comfortable, and then do whatever best produces a let-down. This may be music, silence, looking at a picture of your baby—or Oprah.

When you start to pump, unless your baby has just nursed, you'll probably get very little milk until you get your let-down. Then pump until the milk flow stops. For the first week, don't expect to get much milk; your body has to adjust to producing extra for your pumping sessions. Start on the minimum setting, and dial the pressure up until you're getting milk. If you're using a single pump, pump for five minutes on each side, alternating for as long as you are producing milk. I suggest you use the adapter that lets you pump both

breasts at once—you really don't want a pumping session to last longer than it has to.

How You Can Store Breastmilk

Breastmilk will keep at room temperature for six to
ten hours, depending on how cool your room is. You
can leave it out if you're planning on using it that day
(to eliminate having to heat it). It will keep in the
refrigerator for as long as seven days, and you can
add to it during that period. It will keep in the freezer
for up to four months if your freezer has a separate
door and in a deep freezer for more than six months.
Once thawed, breastmilk can be refrigerated for nine
hours, but not refrozen.

Breastmilk Storage Guidelines				
	Room temp	Refrigerator	Freezer	Deep Freeze
Fresh	10 hrs (66-72°)	8 days	2 weeks (compartment)	6+ months
	4-6 hrs (79°)		4 months (sep. door)	
Thawed	0	24 hrs	0	0

You can store it in plastic bottles, in specially
designed freezer bags that fit into a bottle (regular
disposable bottle bags are too thin for long-term
freezer storage), or in small zipper freezer bags. Be

sure to mark the amount and the date. Freeze in small portions—two to four ounces. (Three ounces seemed the most useful to me.)

When you're ready to use the frozen milk, defrost it in warm running water. Don't use hot water, or you'll compromise the milk's immune boosting effect. Shake it up, as the fat will have risen to the top. If you feed the baby unshaken milk, she'll get all cream, will get full, and may not get enough overall fluid.

Chapter 6

Moving on to Real Food—When Is It Time?

BY THE TIME YOU'RE finally feeling comfortable about breastfeeding or bottle-feeding, people will start asking you whether your baby has started eating solids—probably sooner than the baby actually should.

When to Start with Solids

Several years ago, the recommended age for introducing solid food was four months. Currently, the American Academy of Pediatrics advises that parents wait until their infants are six months old before giving them any food except formula or breastmilk. If you are exclusively breastfeeding, you should definitely wait that long to introduce solids, because even foods as seemingly innocuous as cereal interfere with the efficient absorption of iron from breastmilk.

Reasons for Waiting

By about six months, most babies are physically ready to swallow solid foods. The so-called tongue extrusion reflex—in which most things that go into a baby's mouth are quickly pushed out by his tongue—fades away. An older baby's digestive enzymes have matured to the point where he can fairly efficiently break down solid foods. His intestines have started secreting a protein called immunoglobulin (IgA), which prevents allergens from passing into the bloodstream. It's important to wait for these capacities to develop, because once a breastfed baby starts solids, he may lose some of his protection against infections and allergies.

Be Patient

Besides the health reasons for holding off on solids, there are a few practical ones. Solids will quickly transform the reasonably tolerable smell of a breastfed baby's poop into foul sludge. Cleaning up spit-up stains will become challenging. If you've got a trip planned, take it before you enter the solid food stage; a couple of days' worth of baby food can really weigh down your suitcase. And trust me,

Mindful Mommy

These foods are the most likely to cause an allergic reaction in babies: citrus fruits, tomatoes, strawberries, wheat, corn, soy products, cow's milk, egg whites, shellfish, and peanuts. Be alert for systems of an allergic reaction if you try any of them.

you'll be happier if you can postpone the challenge of feeding a baby squirming on your lap in an airplane seat.

The only reason for jumping the gun is if your baby is at least four months old and is acting like she's going to go ahead and start solids without you. She may be ready if she stares at you when you eat and grabs at your food, mouths all of her toys, can sit up (with support) fairly well, nurses frequently, or drinks huge amounts of formula but still seems hungry. Most importantly, she's ready if she doesn't immediately use her tongue to push out anything that you put into her mouth.

Alexander let me know, in no uncertain terms, that he was ready to eat solids by grabbing the salad and mashed potatoes off of my husband's dinner plate and cramming them into his mouth. Neither of these were exactly the ideal first foods, but we both got the idea.

So wait the six months, if you can. The window for the introduction of solid food is a lot wider than the window for the introduction of the bottle. Alexander had his first taste of solids at five-and-a-half months (back when the recommended starting time was four months) after we returned from a planned trip to Hawaii. My daughter had to wait until after she got over a cold (I didn't want her struggling to swallow with a stuffed nose), again at five-and-a-half months when the experts were suggesting four. My youngest son waited until he was six-and-a-half months, after a trip to Mexico.

Your Baby Is Ready for Solids When . . .

- ✓ He's at least six months old if breastfed or at least four months old if bottle-fed
- ✓ She imitates a vulture when you're eating, ready to pounce on your food
- ✓ He stops sticking his tongue out when his mouth is touched
- ✓ She sits with support and controls her head well enough to lean forward when she wants more food
- ✓ He's almost ready to sit up on his own
- ✓ She indicates she's full when you are feeding her

First "Real" Foods for Baby

Baby won't just eat anything—and they shouldn't! Meals that you are accustomed to eating are probably way too advanced for your baby. So, a better first food than a green salad is rice cereal. Rice is easy to digest and unlikely to cause an allergic reaction. Alternatives, particularly if your baby has a tendency to be constipated, are barley and oat cereal. And keep in mind, wheat should be introduced between six and seven months, to reduce later allergies.

Instant, ready-to-mix rice cereal is widely available, and the standard brands are basically alike. To prepare instant rice cereal, mix about two teaspoons of the cereal with breastmilk or formula or, if you're using a cereal that already includes powdered formula, water. Experiment with the texture to see what your baby prefers, but start out with the mixture a bit soupy, but not so thin it runs off of the spoon.

You can also make rice cereal from scratch, but the downside is that homemade cereals are not iron fortified, and at six months your baby is ready for a boost of iron. The cereal-making process can be as simple (rice plus water cooked into a mush) or as elaborate as you choose. One of the moms in my first mother's group fed her baby only cereal made with brown rice, soaked overnight in spring water with strips of seaweed, and cooked fresh every morning in a pressure cooker. (That seemed a little too Martha-Stewart-meets-Earth-Mother for me, but her baby slept more than mine did, so she had time for such projects. Instant cereal was about all I could handle at the six-month mark.)

It's All in the Wrist

For your baby's first supper, pick a time when he's starting to seem hungry, but not frantically so. Forget about assembling the high chair; he won't be ready for that for a few weeks. Instead, put your baby in an infant seat or on the lap of an available adult,

Mommy Knows Best

Honey is off limits during a baby's first year, even in baked foods. Honey contains botulism spores. These are easily disarmed by a mature digestive system, but can cause severe illness, and even death, in babies.

making sure he is basically upright, with his head tipped slightly back.

Do not put solid foods in a bottle or an infant feeder unless your doctor has told you to do so (which she will suggest only if your child has one of a very small list of medical conditions). It is easy to overfeed using a feeder, unlike a spoon that your baby can easily push away.

Scoop a tiny bit of cereal on an infant or demitasse spoon—or even your own finger—and put it just into the front of your baby's mouth. Don't shove it in; she needs to learn for herself how to get the food off of the spoon and far enough back into her mouth to swallow. Since you're introducing this at a stage when she is mouthing everything in sight, she'll probably open her mouth as soon as the spoon gets close.

Then let your baby do whatever he wants with the cereal. He may try to suck the spoon. He may push the cereal out with his tongue. Matter-of-factly scoop it off of his chin and back into his mouth. My husband, Eric, having worked as an aide feeding people in a nursing home, was great at this part. Eventually, he may swallow and then open his

Mindful Mommy

During the first year, solid food is only a supplement—the baby's primary nutrition source remains breastmilk or formula. Don't panic if it seems like your baby isn't eating all that much.

mouth for another bite. Once he turns away, he's had enough, even if it's only been a few spoonfuls. Respect his appetite, and stop when he's full; don't try to coax in one last bite. Let your baby decide how much he wants to eat. The average baby, once he is eating confidently and has moved to three meals a day, eats the equivalent of one jar of baby food at each meal.

If she starts to get bored with this new game, wipe her off and put away the spoon and bowl, but bring it out again at around the same time the next day. If she balks completely—closes her mouth from the beginning, turns away from the spoon, or just starts screaming—try again tomorrow. If she balks several days in a row, give it up for a few weeks and try again; some babies just aren't ready when you think they should be.

Tricks of the Trade

Be prepared: Most feedings, at first, don't go all that smoothly. Your baby may grab at the spoon—so give him one of his own to hold. My kids grabbed at every bite that went into their mouths, so I was constantly trading spoons with them. He may want to smoosh the cereal with his fingers. Let him—he'll probably suck some off of his fingers, as well. He may refuse to open his mouth; try opening yours wide, and take a bite yourself.

Stuff to have on hand when your baby is ready to try solid food:

- Infant feeding spoon or demitasse spoon
- Big bibs for baby; an apron for you
- Sturdy highchair with a safety strap or infant seat
- Topless plastic cups, preferably with handles; no-spill cups
- Food processor or blender; food grinder
- Washcloths
- Disposable self-stick placemats for restaurant tables or highchair trays
- A plastic mat, towel, or a dog to catch spills
- Portable clip-on highchair for restaurants or visits

This eating thing is supposed to be fun. If the messiness is making you crazy, turn up the heat, strip her down to her diaper, and put a towel or shower curtain (for wider coverage) under her chair.

Moms who have the easiest time with the mess that comes with feeding a baby are the ones who own a dog, preferably a big one, with an omnivorous palate. Such dogs position themselves strategically under the highchair and lap up any spills as soon as they hit the ground. These moms say they wouldn't feed a baby without one. The rest of us have made do with newspapers, towels, a plastic mat, or just a mop. If you're really lucky, and the weather's cooperative, feed your baby outside. Hose down the highchair and area under it afterward. (Remember to remove your baby first.)

Rice Cereal: What's Next?

Stick to rice cereal, once or twice a day, for two weeks or so—or even as long as a month. This food is easy to digest, unlikely to cause allergies, and can be prepared with a thicker consistency as your baby gets more proficient at eating.

Slowly introduce other foods to your baby's diet. "Slowly" is the key word here. Feed your baby a single new food, in tiny portions, for at least three days straight before moving on to another food, and watch for signs of allergic reaction. (Don't serve a mixed food until you've allergy tested most of the ingredients first.) It is much easier to allergy test at the food introduction stage than figure out what caused an allergy later. It's a good idea to keep a chart of what foods you've introduced, and what reaction, if any, you noticed. You can use the Food Introduction Record in the Appendix to keep track of food introductions and your baby's reaction to certain foods.

Mommy Knows Best

Bananas, potatoes, zucchini, sweet potatoes, and peas all mash easily without special processing and make great baby food. If your baby rejects rice cereal, try oatmeal. Although most moms start their babies on rice, most babies like oatmeal even better.

While there is wide agreement that rice cereal is the perfect first food, there is less agreement about what the second food should be. One theory is that the next few foods should be vegetables, not fruits, so your baby doesn't get the idea that all food is sweet. The other theory holds the opposite; that fruits, because of their sweetness, are more likely to interest your baby, and should be introduced before vegetables.

Both theories made sense to me, so I alternated. Every few weeks I introduced a new type of cereal into the mix as well. My favorite second foods were bananas and avocados (both are easily mashed with a fork), then squash (usually a big hit) and applesauce. In general, the order doesn't matter that much.

Top Ten First Foods

1. Rice cereal
2. Oat cereal
3. Barley cereal
4. Applesauce
5. Bananas
6. Avocado
7. Pears
8. Squash
9. Sweet potatoes
10. Peas

Baby Food Safety Tips

- Don't feed your baby directly from the jar. Once saliva enzymes from the spoon touch the food, they break down nutrients and speed up spoilage. To avoid waste, spoon a meal's worth of food into a bowl. If you must feed from the jar, throw what's left away.

- Refrigerate unused food immediately.
- Don't keep an open, refrigerated jar of baby food longer than two days—even if it tastes fine to you, bacteria can make your baby sick.
- If you're giving your baby food from a can, either run the can opener through the dishwasher, or use one reserved for this purpose (not the one you use to open the dog food).
- Give your baby only pasteurized juices.

Meat and Dairy

At around eight months, you can, if you'd like, give your baby his first taste of meat. But don't panic if those little jarred meats never make it into your baby's mouth. The only one around here who ever ate the baby food turkey was our cat. You can try mixing meats with pureed vegetables, or grind up meat from your family's dinner, which at least smells better than the jarred meats. Or you can just wait until your baby is old enough to pick up a bit of chicken and chew it for himself. Meat is not necessary in the first year; your baby is getting all the protein he needs from the formula or breastmilk that he is drinking. Wait until your baby is at least twelve months old before feeding him dairy products. Cow's milk can cause intestinal blood loss and subsequent anemia.

The Vegetarian Baby

A healthy vegetarian diet that also includes milk and eggs can easily meet all your baby's nutritional needs. A vegetarian diet should include lots of iron-rich foods (dried fruits, beans, and fortified cereal), and a daily multivitamin with iron (make sure this is stored out of reach of your baby; iron poisoning can be fatal). It should also incorporate frequent high-calorie snacks, like nut butters (hold off on peanut butter until after your child is twelve months old) and avocados.

Meeting all of your baby's nutritional needs is less easily accomplished on a vegan (vegetable foods only) diet. Vitamin B12 can only be supplied by animal products, and it is also difficult to provide sufficient calcium, vitamin D, and riboflavin, which originate largely, but not exclusively, in dairy products. It can be especially difficult for infants on a vegan diet to consume the quantity of food required to provide the necessary amounts of these essential nutrients. Infants also need much higher levels of fat in their diet—necessary for proper brain development—than adults, and a vegan diet is typically low fat.

Mommy Must

Wash and save your baby food jars. You can use them to store homemade baby food, a meal-sized portion of food for travel, or a serving's worth of dry baby cereal; just add liquid when you're ready.

The Poop Problem

Constipation is not uncommon in the early weeks of introducing solid food. You're giving your baby something a lot harder to digest than breast-milk or formula, and the most typical first foods—rice cereal, banana, and applesauce—are binding. Sometimes, adding fluids (a bottle or cup of water a day) is enough to solve the problem. You can also feed your baby a little prune juice, or switch from rice cereal and applesauce to oat cereal and pureed pears.

Learn to Be Label-Savvy

When you're shopping for baby food, you would think a jar of pureed plums would contain, simply, plums. But you can't assume that—check the label. In the past, baby food companies would regularly add sugar and thickeners (like tapioca starch) to their products, reasoning that babies preferred sweeter, smoother foods. This may be true, but may not be the preference to reinforce. After a fuss in the press a few years ago, jarred baby foods, at least those designed as first foods, became purer. You should still check the label, however, in particular for foods labeled "fruit desserts" or "stage three" foods. If the label says that the product includes fructose or dextrose or maltodextrins, don't be fooled—these are all different forms of sugars.

Be on the lookout, too, for corn products, including corn syrup, as a sweetener and cornstarch as a thickener. These can trigger allergies in a sensitive baby.

The Ups and Downs of Drinking from a Cup

You can begin teaching your baby to drink from a cup at about the same time you start solids, or even a little sooner.

Offer sips of breastmilk, formula, or water from a cup beginning at about five months—not for nutrition, but for practice. Or, let her have a drink from your glass of water. Put the cup to her lips and tip it until just a tiny sip pours out. Since most of it, at first, will trickle down her chin, try it when you're getting ready to change her clothes anyway. Or hold cup practice at bath time.

When your baby starts eating solids, he can also have small amounts of juice, preferably mixed with water. Keep the amount of juice small (less than four ounces a day), or he may fill up on juice and not get the other nutrients that he needs.

Mindful Mommy

Watch out for and avoid artificial flavors and colors (red #40, yellow #5, etc.). These may cause unpredictable allergic reactions, and there is some unconfirmed evidence implicating them in neurological disorders.

There are three basic kinds of infant cups, and you'll eventually want to get your baby used to all three of them. She should learn to drink from a cup without a top, controlling the flow with her lips. Like eating, this is a skill that has to be practiced. You will also want her to drink occasionally from a cup with a spouted lid; for example, when she's eating finger foods in her highchair and you want her to have a drink available, but don't want her to soak herself if you step away. These cups allow the liquid to flow out in a small stream. The baby still has to control the flow herself, but the liquid pours out fairly slowly if the cup is tipped over.

You'll also want your baby to drink from a no-spill cup. These cups have valves inside their spouts, and don't spill even if shaken. They're great for the stroller, the car, or even wandering around the house. But the experience of drinking from them is closer to that of sucking from a bottle than drinking from a cup, so they shouldn't be your baby's only cups.

Slurping and Swallowing— As Your Baby Grows

Between approximately eight to ten months, most babies will be pretty proficient at slurping and swallowing, and you'll be used to the routine. You've allergy tested a fair number of foods and have a fairly long list of things that your baby can and will eat. He's opening his mouth like a little bird whenever he sees the spoon, and you're getting a lot more of his food in his mouth than on his clothes. Daily menus are easy—a few bowls of cereal, a few servings of pureed fruits and vegetables, and you're set.

Then your baby pulls a fast one. "No more mush!" her pursed lips seem to say as she knocks the spoon out of your hand and pureed carrots spatter across the floor. Your baby is sick of goop.

However, he has only a few teeth, and is not nearly ready to handle a knife and fork. You can't expect to pass him the steak and potatoes just yet. Well, maybe the potatoes.

One Lump or Two?

One option is moving to lumpier baby foods. The prepared versions marked "stage three" are designated for older babies. If you are making them yourself, don't puree them as long and leave in some chunks. The change in texture and the more complex tastes of these foods may get your little bird opening her mouth again.

Or not. My kids were used to slurping baby mush, and food for older babies made them gag and frequently throw up much of their meal. They were ready for something to get their teeth into (or gums, actually; children don't really use their teeth to chew until they are well over two), and the mushy/chewy combination was too confusing for them. What's a parent to do?

Cereal Strategies

Grab the Cheerios, or, to be brand neutral, oat cereal rings. Scatter a few on your baby's tray, and he'll try to pick them up and put them in his mouth. These may entertain him enough for you to slip in a few spoonfuls of mush in between bites.

Cheerios are a popular food for nascent self-feeders for a number of reasons. First, they are made of oats, not wheat, so allergies are unlikely to be an issue. Second, they are spit soluble and quickly soften into easy-to-swallow mush. Unlike peas, they are hard to choke on and more likely to stick to your baby's mouth than to be inhaled. Third, they give your baby great practice at picking things up with her thumb and forefinger. This pincer grasp is a developmental milestone (see Chapter 12) that she is likely to be working on around the same time she becomes interested in self-feeding.

Another option is a teething biscuit. There are a number of varieties available, or you can make your own. Read the labels; some have a lot more sugar than others. Teething biscuits dissolve into mush as your baby gums them. But don't leave your baby

Mommy Knows Best

At the age of six months, your child will begin needing fluoride in her diet to ensure healthy development of her teeth. Check with your local water department to see if your water is fluoridated. If it isn't, you can purchase fluoridated bottled water marketed for infants, have fluoridated spring water delivered, or ask your pediatrician to prescribe fluoride drops.

alone with one, since large pieces can break off and pose a choking danger.

Keeping It Interesting with Finger Foods

There is no reason your self-feeder should have a boring diet. Provide him with a variety of foods to enhance nutrition and give him important experience with different tastes and textures.

Finger foods must be soft, break down into small pieces, and be easy to swallow. There are a host of fruits that meet those criteria—cantaloupe, peaches, pears, plums, kiwis, avocados, and even apples, if they are first steamed or poached (slice them, add a spoonful of water, and cook them in the microwave). Just remove any peels and pits and cut into bite-sized pieces. For vegetables like broccoli, squash, and carrots, steam or boil them until reasonably soft.

Pasta makes a great early finger food—just pick small shapes and cook them until soft. Serve it plain, with tomato sauce, or with pesto. A garlicky pesto was an early favorite with my babies. Perhaps

Mommy Must

Whatever finger food you're serving, give your baby only a few pieces at a time, and as soon as throwing the food on the floor becomes more interesting than putting it in her mouth, consider her mealtime finished.

that shouldn't have been a surprise, as studies have shown that nursing babies prefer breastmilk after the mother has eaten garlic.

Breakfast foods are also good finger foods—any time of the day. Whole-grain waffles (purchased frozen and heated in the toaster), pancakes (use a whole-grain mix, make a batch, and freeze them; they are easily reheated in the microwave), and French toast (for babies under twelve months, make it with separated egg yolks mixed with formula or breastmilk) are all good options. You can spread any of these with a fruit or vegetable puree to bump up the nutrition.

The finger food stage can start as early as six months or not until several months later. It depends on your child's personality, for one. Babies with strong individual preferences and a lust for independence will move into this stage earlier than more easygoing babies. It also depends on the environment. If you don't mind a mess, your baby probably gets her hands into her cereal regularly, and that has already become her first finger food experience. If neatness is important to you and you are quick to wipe up spills, your baby may have gotten the message that she should keep her hands out of the way at mealtime.

Either way, by twelve months, your baby will probably do most of his feeding himself. Most of that will be with his fingers—although he may begin to experiment with using a spoon, he probably won't be very successful yet.

Finger Food Options—
for Six-to-Eight-Month Olds

1. Cheerios
2. Zwieback
3. Bananas
4. Soft-cooked vegetables
5. Bagels
6. Avocado slices
7. Arrowroot cookies
8. Peeled carrot (to gum on, before teeth emerge)
9. Mashed potatoes
10. Graham crackers

Finger Foods Options—
for Nine-to-Twelve-Month Olds

1. Cheerios
2. Egg noodles
3. Rice cakes
4. Toast
5. Tofu
6. Scrambled egg yolks
7. Rice
8. Small meatballs
9. Avocado slices
10. Ripe peaches

Since a baby's airway is the size of the tip of her pinky, you should always serve finger foods under constant adult supervision. Only give finger foods to a child who is sitting up, not lying down or walking around. Be sure that all finger foods are soft and cut into small pieces.

Setting the Pace

Meals at the finger-feeding stage will be messy and may take a long time. Resist the temptation to step in and neatly tuck each bite of food into your baby's mouth. Eating isn't just about nutrition at this point—it's about learning. This is your baby's time to learn to like different tastes and textures; to learn to get food from the bowl to his mouth, gums, or throat; and to learn about when to eat and when to stop.

Chapter 7

Diaper Decisions

YOU MIGHT THINK THAT you are expected to know all about taking care of a baby, from washing his hair to cutting his toenails. And many mothers think that the most important thing to know is how to give your baby a bath. The bath to diaper-changing ratio suggests that you'll need to know a lot more about diapering than how to bathe him—but it's important to know how and when to do both!

The Scoop on Diaper Duty

In your baby's first few days, her poop will look like tar—black, sticky, and hard to remove. This is meconium, a thick, dark green or black paste that fills a baby's intestines in utero, and it must be eliminated before she can digest normally. If you're lucky, she'll have eliminated most of the meconium in the hospital. If not, you'll be wiping it off at home. It's sticky stuff, and may not come off with plain water; try a little baby oil on a cotton ball.

In the transitional stage, your baby's bowel movements will turn yellow-green. If you're breastfeeding, after your milk comes in your baby's poop will resemble seeded, slightly runny Dijon mustard. If you're formula-feeding, it will be more tan, and thicker than peanut butter.

The most amazing thing about this bodily function is how noisy it can be from such a small person. There you are, holding your precious, dozing baby as relatives coo over how sweet he is, when you hear the sound of a volcano erupting. It's definitely a conversation stopper, and a clue to run, not walk, to the changing table.

Typically, your baby will dirty several diapers a day. But she may have bowel movements as often as ten times a day or as infrequently as once a week. Both are normal. The ten-times-a-day baby does not have diarrhea and the once-a-week baby is not constipated (unless the poop, when it comes, arrives in pellets).

Be forewarned: You will need lots of diapers. I was perfectly happy to let the nurses deal with diapering at the hospital. The nurses in the hospital whisked those disposable diapers on and off faster than the eye could see. Once you get home, however, things aren't quite so simple. First, you have to choose sides—are you going to be on Team Cloth, or Team Disposable?

There are women who can argue about their diaper choices for hours. One concern is the impact to the environment: disposables become solid waste that must be disposed of in landfills; cloth diapers use energy and water for laundering, and, if you're using a diaper service, transporting. The other concern is the health of the baby: cloth diapers are more natural and you're likely to change them more often; disposables keep baby drier, but leak synthetic pellets when they get overloaded. Then there is the middle road—disposable diapers that don't contain chemically synthesized absorbents, called Tushies.

Team Cloth

When I left the hospital with my first child, I thought I was going to play for Team Cloth. A stack of cloth diapers, fresh from the diaper service, was waiting for me. I used them exclusively for about a week. During that week, I washed countless loads of laundry, because every time Alexander pooped (which was often) it exploded through his clothes. By week two, I was using disposables at night. By week three, I was using disposables whenever I took my baby out, and by week four I was pretty much using disposables all the time. At week six, I canceled the diaper service.

Mommy Knows Best

After removing messy cloth diapers, rinse them in the toilet. Keep wet diapers in a diaper pail half-full of water and ½ cup of vinegar. Put diapers in washing machine and run spin cycle to remove excess water. Reset to full cycle in hot water, using mild detergent and bleach. Add ½ cup vinegar to final rinse. Machine dry on high or line dry.

But ever since, I have been impressed by women who used cotton diapers exclusively. I feel like I tried out for their team, but didn't make the cut, so somehow they must be more talented than I am.

I might have had more success with cloth had I started out with disposables for the first month or two, then switched to cloth when the poops become less explosive and less frequent. I might have had more success using cloth with my next two babies, since they had really dirty diapers only once a week instead of five times a day.

It also turns out that, in spite of a diapering class at the hospital, I had no real idea of how to make cloth diapers work.

Applied Skills

PREFOLD DIAPERS

I was instructed to fold the supposedly "pre-folded" diaper into thirds lengthwise (prefolds have a thick center and thinner edge sections and are rect-angular in shape; nonprefolds are squarer and of uni-form thickness).

Set up

Fasten

Then I was instructed to open it out at the corners, wrap it so it overlapped at the sides of my baby, then cover the whole thing with a diaper wrap. In practice, this may be about the least effective folding method.

SQUARE DIAPERS

Instead, forget about prefolds and just fold a standard square diaper into a triangle. Put one point between the legs and pull the other two points around the side to meet it near the middle of the belly.

Set up   **Fasten**

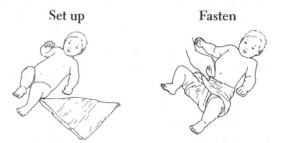

DIAPERING WITH A TWIST

Or fold the diaper in thirds, but then twist the part that goes between your baby's legs to make it extra thick where it counts. You can fold the diaper down in the front before wrapping it around your baby to give a boy baby extra thickness where he'll need it most.

You can also use two diapers. Place one, folded in half or in thirds, between the baby's legs. Wrap the second diaper on top (using whichever method), and pin only the outside diaper to hold everything in place.

Set up **Fasten**

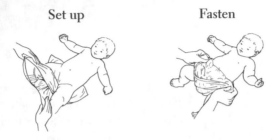

Even better than the prefolded or unfolded square diapers, are the contoured diapers (kind of like a fitted sheet). These don't need to be folded—they are designed to fit easily around your baby's butt. Unfortunately, these aren't commonly offered by diaper services.

Once you've figured out how to fold your baby's diaper, you can fasten it with diaper pins, clips, special tape, or a wrap that fastens with snaps or Velcro. If you're using pins, open them up and stick them in a bar of soap before you start the diaper change, and make sure they are out of baby's reach.

Mindful Mommy

Use a cloth diaper or a waterproof flannel mattress pad as a changing pad when you're away from home. The cute little changing pads that come with diaper bags are so waterproof that any accidents run right off the pad onto the couch/chair/lap you're changing him on.

Reasons to Use Cloth Diapers

- Cloth diapers have a hundred other uses, including peek-a-boo, burping rag, and, sooner than you might think, dust rag and silver polisher.
- You'll be more attentive to your baby's needs, since you'll have to change her diaper more quickly when she wets.
- Kids may potty train earlier.
- They are less expensive than disposables, so you save money.
- Fewer chemicals are touching your baby's skin.
- They may be environmentally correct.

Team Disposable

One reason disposables are probably more popular is that putting them on is more intuitive. Open one up with the tapes or Velcro tags underneath your baby, put his bottom in the middle of the diaper, bring the front of the diaper up between his legs, and fasten the tabs at his waist. However, there are a few tricks to diapering with disposables:

- While your baby still has her umbilical cord, fold the top of the diaper down to turn it into a bikini before fastening.
- Make sure the leg edges are turned out, not folded back under the elastic. This creates a better seal.

- If your disposables fasten with adhesive tapes, make sure not to get anything on the adhesive—lotion, water, or powder will ruin their stickiness. If your disposables fasten with Velcro tabs, don't pull the tabs too hard, or they might rip off.
- When you're diapering a boy, make sure his penis is pointed down in the center of the diaper. If you accidentally diaper his penis up, or tucked out a leg edge, you will end up with a wet lap.

Even though today's disposables are unlikely to leak until they weigh more than your baby, change them once they get a little squishy. Otherwise, the little pellets of superabsorbent gel burst out of the diaper and are pretty much impossible to get off of your baby's skin unless you give her a full bath.

Reasons to use disposable diapers include:

- Disposables are required by most day-care centers and preferred by babysitters.
- They're less bulky, so your baby's clothes will fit better.
- You have less financial commitment up front, and you don't need pins or wraps.
- Used diapers go right out to the trash.
- You'll have fewer changes and less laundry to do.
- Fewer changes also mean there is a better chance your baby will sleep all night.

Learn about Different Diapering Strategies

Make sure you have everything you need within reach before you put your baby on the changing table, countertop, bed, or floor to change him. Use the dirty diaper to do as much preliminary wiping as you can before you bring out the clean cloths or wipes.

Try not to look disgusted; you want your baby to think getting her diaper changed is fun. Sing, spin a mobile, or hold a toy in your mouth—anything to keep your baby entertained and on her back. Clean the baby's bottom with plain water using an infant washcloth, cut-up towel, soft paper towel, or cotton balls for the first month. Save commercial diaper wipes for later, as they may irritate your baby's skin.

For a girl, make sure you wipe front to back, using a clean section of washcloth or piece of cotton each time, to prevent spreading poop to the vagina. Although you don't typically need to clean the inside of the lips of the vulva, sometimes it seems as if poop is in every fold, back and front.

For a boy, toss an extra diaper over his penis while you're cleaning him. This reduces the chance

Mommy Must

To keep things simple, use distraction as much as possible. Have a special toy your baby only gets at diaper time, making sure it's lightweight in case she drops it on herself, sing special songs, or make faces.

of getting a fountain in the face. This isn't a bad precaution when changing a girl, either!

When you're done diapering, dump whatever is loose from the dirty diaper into the toilet. This goes for disposable diapers, too. Their biggest environmental hazard may not be the amount of paper in the diapers; a larger concern is the problems caused by leaching bacteria. Dry your baby with a clean washcloth or cloth diaper. When you're done, wash your hands well.

Diapering gets more challenging as your baby gets more control over his body and can kick away your hands, flip over, and, eventually, try to stand up. If he's persistent in wriggling, move the scene of operation to a washable rug on the floor. I use washable nonskid bathroom rugs as area rugs in my children's rooms. You may have to swing a leg over his torso to gently pin him to the floor during some of the wrigglier stages. And once your baby learns to stand up, you may have to learn to change his diaper while he's vertical.

Whether you go cloth or disposable, you will spend a lot of time with diapers over the next couple of years. Over time, you'll discover what brands and

Mommy Knows Best

Put additional materials to good use! Cut up a cloth diaper into four squares and use the squares as an extra liner for either cloth or disposable diapers at night.

methods work best for you and your baby. Whatever brand or method you go with, make sure your changing surface (changing table or empty counter) is tall enough so you don't hurt your back when bending over it. While you're perfecting your technique, there are a few things all changing stations need:

- If you plan on using disposables, keep one bag in the current size, and one bag of the next size up waiting in the wings.
- If you're using cloth, you'll need three to four dozen in each size.
- You'll need three to six diaper wraps to go over the cloth diapers.
- Use washcloths for the first month, before switching to diaper wipes.
- Get a diaper pail designed for whichever type of diapers you're using.
- Get a variety of changing pads—one for the changing table, one for traveling, and a larger, waterproof pad for naked time.
- Keep two pad covers in rotation—one on the pad, one in the wash.
- Have cream or ointment for diaper rash; odds are you'll need it eventually.
- Invest in a waterproof flannel crib pad or disposable bed pads (those blue and white ones). You'll need them now, and they're a good idea to keep for the crib-to-bed transition.

Here are some strategies to improve the quality of time spent diapering:

- If your changing table has a strap, slip your hand between your baby's belly and the clip before you try to fasten it to avoid pinching your baby's delicate skin.
- Speed counts—the faster you can get your baby diapered and dressed, the happier you're both likely to be.
- Accuracy counts—if the diaper isn't lined up correctly on your baby before you fasten it, it will probably leak.
- Put a towel or extra cloth diaper under your boy or girl baby and another one over your boy baby while you're changing. Babies do pee when their diapers are off.
- Stash several special toys in a box near your diaper table and let your child see these toys only at changing time.

Diaper Rash Reality

Diaper rash can be as mild as a little redness or as severe as bleeding sores. Some babies seem to get them all the time; others hardly ever. Peak diaper rash times are when babies start to eat solid foods, when they sleep through the night in a dirty diaper, and when they are taking antibiotics. The best way to treat it is to prevent it.

Change diapers frequently (immediately if they're messy). Expose your baby's bottom to air as often as you can. When your baby's an infant, this is pretty easy. In a warm room, put her belly down on a disposable absorbent pad (the kind you sat on in the hospital) or use a waterproof crib pad with a cloth diaper on top of it. Once your baby is mobile, it is less likely she'll stay put. If it's summer, let her run around barebottomed outside. If it's winter, you might consider heating up your bathroom and giving her a little extra naked time after her bath.

What you don't have to do to prevent diaper rash is slather on ointment with every diaper change.

If you notice a little redness—the beginnings of diaper rash—begin treating it immediately. Don't just hope it will go away on it's own; it's likely to get worse, becoming a lot more uncomfortable for your baby and a lot harder for you to treat. Also understand that, left untreated, a simple case of diaper rash can become a yeast infection, which is a lot harder to get rid of than ordinary diaper rash. A yeast infection typically comes on quickly and intensely, characterized by a bright red rash around the diaper

Mindful Mommy

Baby powder isn't much help in protecting against or curing diaper rash, and talc-based powders can be particularly dangerous when inhaled. Cornstarch powders clump up in skin folds and can encourage the growth of yeast. When carefully applied, powder is not necessarily bad, but it doesn't serve any great purpose, either.

area, with small red pimples here and there in the surrounding areas.

If that sounds too messy for you, and it's warm outside, let him roll around on a towel on the grass. Or, put a cloth diaper down in your stroller, sit your baby on top of it, and go for a long walk.

What about an Ointment?

Ointments come into play when your baby has diaper rash and can't be naked. These are typically oil based (such as Vaseline, A&D ointment, or plain olive oil) or zinc-oxide based (Desitin, Balmex, or Johnson & Johnson, for example). The ointment creates a barrier, protecting your baby's skin. To work, it has to be spread on thickly. If standard ointments are ineffective, you might ask your drugstore to order a thick cream called Triple Paste or Aquafor. Both are hard to find and expensive, but some moms swear by them. Others reach for Bag Balm, an ointment intended for use on cows with chapped udders. Bag Balm, used to treat a variety of skin problems, soothes soreness and inhibits bacteria growth, but it is only FDA approved for use on animals.

If you suspect a yeast infection, ask your pediatrician to prescribe an antifungal ointment or use an over-the-counter antifungal cream, like Lotrimin. However, if your doctor prescribes a combination steroid-antifungal cream, like Lotrisone, only use it as long as recommended. Do not use it as a regular diaper cream, because the steroid can lead to serious side effects in children, including thinning of the skin.

In Hawaii, where the humid climate makes diaper rash a real problem, moms use pure cocoa butter to prevent diaper rash. Cocoa butter is available at most drugstores. It comes in solid bars or sticks and must be warmed. Put it in a jar, then sit the jar on a sunny windowsill or in a bowl of warm water. If you live near a grocer that caters to a Latino community, you have access to another remedy—plantain leaves. Crush fresh leaves and use them to line your baby's diaper.

If you're battling diaper rash and using home-washed cloth diapers, add vinegar to the rinse water. Diaper services often treat their diapers in this way as a standard practice or will do so upon request.

If you're using disposable diapers, consider peeling off the outside plastic cover and fastening a cloth diaper around it. That combination will prevent leaks while allowing air to get through.

If your baby has graduated to wipes, you should go back to using plain water to clean your baby's bottom while she has the rash. Diaper wipes may make the rash worse.

Mommy Must

Think about curing diaper rash the same way you would prevent it—by keeping wetness away and exposing the irritated area to plenty of air.

How to Care for Sensitive Areas

The first time I changed a diaper and saw a spot of blood, I panicked. However, in the early days red spots are not a concern. They can come from urates, which are normal crystals in a baby's urine that turn to a salmon color on the diaper. In girls, spots within the first week home may also be a small amount of bloody vaginal discharge caused by the mother's hormones.

Penis Care

If your son is circumcised, don't clean his penis at all for the first four days. After that, wipe it gently with a wet cotton ball, then pat it dry with a clean cloth diaper. You'll probably be given a tube of sterile petroleum jelly from the hospital. For the first four days or so after the circumcision, squeeze some onto a gauze pad and cap the pad over the tip of the penis every time you change him. This keeps it from sticking to the diaper. After a few days, you may see a yellowish discharge that forms a crust. This is normal, as are a few spots of blood. If the penis oozes blood, call the doctor.

If your son is not circumcised, don't retract his foreskin for cleaning; if you force it, you could cause bleeding and scarring. Normal bathing will keep him clean.

Bellybutton Care

Your baby's bellybutton needs special attention until the cord dries up and falls off (usually two but perhaps as long as five weeks), because this area can get infected. To prevent infection, keep her bellybutton dry and clean, and expose it to air as much as possible.

That doesn't necessarily mean you shouldn't immerse your baby in water until the cord is gone, only that you shouldn't cover the cord area until it is completely dry. If you see any signs of redness or pus, however, don't immerse him, and call your pediatrician.

You'll probably be told to swab around the base of the cord with a cotton swab dipped in rubbing alcohol several times a day. This has a dual purpose—alcohol both kills bacteria and dries out the cord. Although recent studies have shown that water may work just as well, your doctor will probably recommend alcohol.

You may see a few drops of blood as the cord detaches. This is normal, as is a little yellow discharge. Redness on the skin around the bellybutton or oozing pus are not normal, and if you see either, call your doctor immediately.

Chapter 8

Baths, Grooming, and Naked Time

INFANTS DON'T GET ALL that dirty, so one bath a week is plenty until she's eating solid foods and crawling in the dirt. Just be sure to wash her face, hands, neck, and diaper area daily. If your baby likes her bath, you can bathe her every day, as long as you limit her bath to no more than ten minutes.

Bath Time Basics

Who are we kidding? The first bath is a major photo opportunity, and you'll probably want to do it sooner rather than later. There are a couple of approaches, and you'll discover, with practice, which method works best for you and your baby.

Getting the Bath Time Gear You'll Need

The first few baths are relatively simple—you're just concentrating on keeping your baby warm, making him feel secure, and getting him clean. As he grows, of course, toys and boats and ducks will take more room in the tub than he does. In the meantime, stock up on some simple, yet highly recommended, bath aids.

- Cotton balls (for cleaning eyes and ears)
- Plastic cup or spray bottle
- Soft brush
- Baby washcloths (lots, for washing, warmth, and play)
- Several towels
- Giant bath sponge (for baby to lie on, or use another towel)
- Baby soap or no-tear shampoo (the two are pretty much interchangeable) or mild glycerin bar soap
- Baby bathtub, dishpan, or clean sink
- Nonskid mat (for use in the adult tub)
- Foam faucet cover (for adult tub)

The Skinny on a Sponge Bath

If you decide that your baby's first bath should be a sponge bath, give yourself plenty of time to figure out exactly where you're going to conduct this operation. You don't want to be running around the house with a naked baby trying to decide where to bathe her. Your best choice is a counter next to the sink, if your counter is big enough. This has several advantages: Cleanup will be easy since it's waterproof, it's high enough to keep you from wrecking your back, it provides a ready source of warm water, and it makes it easier to rinse your baby's hair.

You'll also need something soft to lay your baby on. A thick, folded bath towel is fine. If you have a baby bathtub that came with a thick contoured sponge, save the tub for later, but place the sponge on the counter.

Make sure you have everything that you need within reach. Along with several big towels, you'll need:

- At least two washcloths (you don't want to wipe a spot of milk from his face with the same washcloth you just used to wipe his backside)
- Cotton balls or another clean washcloth for his eyes
- Baby soap or mild bar soap (like Neutrogena)
- A clean diaper
- Clean clothes
- Diaper rash ointment, if you're using it
- A plastic cup

In order to get started, strip the baby down to her diaper and lay her on the towel. Cover her with the other towel; you'll uncover only the piece of baby you're washing at the moment.

Wipe inside the corners of his eyes, from the inside out, using a clean cotton ball or different corner of the washcloth for each eye. You can use cotton balls to wipe his ear folds, as well. But don't try to wash inside the ear canal, even if you see wax; the wax protects the inner ear.

To wash her hair, wet it with the washcloth, add a dab of soap, and gently massage the entire scalp, including the soft spots. You don't really need a special baby shampoo; liquid baby bath is an all-purpose cleaner at this stage. Then hold your baby so her head, supported by one hand, is tipped slightly back over the sink. Using the plastic cup, pour warm water back over her head, avoiding her eyes. If some soap does get into her eyes, wipe them with plain, warm water; she'll open her eyes once the soap is gone.

Next, take off his diaper and wash his bottom and genitals. If you're bathing a girl, remember to always wash from front to back. Finish by sitting him up, leaning him forward on your hand as if you're going to burp him, and wash his back. Check to make sure all the soap is rinsed off, then dry him with a clean towel, again paying particular attention to the creases in his neck.

Time for the Little Tub

When you're ready to get your baby off the counter and into the tub, you don't need an official baby bathtub. You can bathe your baby in a clean dishpan

Mindful Mommy

When washing your baby, pay special attention to all the creases around his neck, which may be filled with gunk. With a newborn, this gunk is likely to be skin cells sloughing off; with an older baby, the gunk is likely to be dried food. Either way, bath time is a great time to help him get rid of this gunk!

or even the sink itself. When I had my son Alexander, my hospital supplies (the spritz bottle, soap and shampoo, and a couple of ice packs) were handed to me in a tiny pink plastic basin, about two-thirds the size of a normal dishpan. The nurse advised me to save the basin, as it made a perfect baby bath. It looked impossibly small, but it worked perfectly and meant one less large, primary-colored plastic object cluttering up my house.

Whatever type of tub you choose, think of your back when you're positioning it. Having the tub in the sink or up on the counter will be easier to manage than crouching over it on the floor. When I had two kids to bathe, I discovered that the baby tub a friend had lent me hooked solidly across our big tub. If yours doesn't fit well, and you're trying to bathe two kids at once, put the baby tub with its stopper unplugged right inside the big tub—there should be room left for your older child.

Gather up all your supplies while your baby is still dressed. Line the baby tub with something soft (a bath sponge or a towel) and fill it with only two or three inches of lukewarm water; test the temperature on the inside of your wrist or elbow. The idea here is that most of your baby's body and all of her face should be well above the water line. You'll keep her warm by layering extra washcloths over her stomach and pouring warm water on them regularly. (This is a great job to give a sibling.)

Try these bath time tips for improving bath time efficiency, safety, and fun:

- Turn your hot-water heater to a low setting (about 120°F) to avoid dangerous burns.
- Put liquid baby soap into a clean pump dispenser for one-handed use.
- Save the spray bottle the hospital gave you for cleaning your perineum and use it to rinse your baby's hair.
- Bring on the washcloths—the more, the merrier. Besides the one you're using for washing, spread a few others across your baby to keep him warm.
- Pat your baby dry. Don't rub; rubbing can irritate delicate baby skin.
- Heat the towels in the dryer—your baby will love the snuggly warmth.
- The kitchen sink makes a great place for a baby bath, if you have a spray hose and faucet that turns out of the way and all the dishes are done.

Another option is to bathe with your baby. It's a lot easier on your back than leaning over the tub,

Mommy Must

Make your baby comfortable in the baby bath or sink and reduce the chance he'll slide around. Put a folded towel or special-purpose bath sponge on the bottom before you put your baby in the water. If you can keep your baby from getting scared, he'll be much more likely to enjoy bath time!

and you're bound to get wet anyway. (If you have a hard time finding enough time for your own bath in a normal day, this idea is for you!) But don't forget the logistical workings of this option—it's a two-person job. One person gets in the tub first, then the other one hands off the baby. (Reverse the procedure on the way out.) If you have your spouse or loved one there to help, this is a great choice for bathing and bonding with your baby.

Graduating to the Big Tub

Your baby is ready to graduate to a regular bathtub once she can sit steadily without support (usually sometime after six months). When your baby is ready to graduate from the infant tub to the big tub, start out by placing the infant tub inside the big tub for a few baths to get her used to the transition.

You'll find that baby stores sell bath seats or rings for this transition stage. These will give your baby extra support, but probably aren't worth a trip to buy them. Your baby won't use a bath ring for long; as soon as he starts crawling, he'll want to explore the tub. A bath ring or seat may also give you a false sense of confidence. Even when your baby is in a bath ring

Mommy Knows Best

Babies are slippery when wet! They are less likely to slip when held by a big hand, so if bigger hands than yours are available, this might be the time to call them into service.

or seat, you need to stay within grabbing distance—these devices don't keep a baby from tipping over and slipping under the water.

Since a towel or sponge on the bottom of a regular tub will slide all over, get a nonskid mat if your baby doesn't seems to like sitting on the bathtub's hard surface. This will be softer to sit on, as well as safer.

Bath Toys Make It Fun

Your baby will be interested in bath toys when she is old enough to be in a big tub, but keep them simple—a few things that float and a cup that pours water are plenty. Try a nylon bath puff, washcloth, floating plastic book, spray bottle, rubber ducky, boats, bath puppet, or a sibling!

Cradle Cap Explained

When you're washing your baby's head, you may see thick, yellow scales. This is cradle cap, and, although it looks pretty yucky, it's benign. You could let it go away on its own, or try this instead: Rub baby oil or olive oil onto the scalp, let it soak for a few hours, then scrub the cradle cap away with a baby hair brush, baby toothbrush, or nail brush, followed by a dandruff shampoo to get the oil out. You'll have to scrub harder than you think. Don't worry; you won't hurt your baby. I tried for weeks to softly brush off my son's case of cradle cap (since he was a bald baby it looked particularly disgusting) with no success. Then my much more experienced babysitter took brush in hand and vigorously scrubbed it away—without a whimper from Alex.

Nail Trimming Truth

Of all the baby-care tasks, nothing seems to panic parents more than the idea of cutting their baby's nails. My daughter Nadya was born with talons. During her first day of life, I kept staring at them, knowing I really needed to cut them, but wondering how I could do it without cutting off her tiny fingers. The pediatrician came in the next day to check her. She borrowed my manicure scissors and trimmed Nadya's nails in about thirty seconds—experience does count.

Some parents swear by chewing off their baby's nails. This isn't hard to do, because the nails are so soft. The advantage of this is that you don't risk cutting your baby with scissors, but the disadvantage is that you risk tearing the nail down into the skin. I could never bring myself to do this. I don't bite my own nails, and it seemed really strange to consider biting my baby's.

You could avoid the whole issue and put your baby into cotton mittens, but odds are your baby isn't going to like wearing those for long. And frankly, nail cutting is just more traumatic for parents than it is for babies. If you do accidentally nick your child, it really won't hurt all that much and will heal quickly.

Clippers or Scissors?

Seems to me that parents are evenly divided between clippers and scissors. Clippers seem safer than scissors, but can actually cause more damage. The best guide is probably what you're more comfortable using on your own nails—as I said, experience counts. And you may discover, as I did, that your own manicure scissors are actually less likely to draw blood than blunt-tipped infant nail scissors. The blunt tip does keep you from stabbing your baby, but that isn't so much of a risk. The bigger problem is that the blades of baby scissors tend to be a little thicker and difficult to slip easily under your baby's nails, making it more likely that you'll pinch skin.

Trim Time

Wait until your baby is in a deep sleep when you're learning to trim nails. This means his arms and legs flop when lifted, and his hand is resting open, not in a fist. Hold the scissors or clippers in one hand; with the other, pull the tip of his finger down away from the nail. You should now have better access to the nail, so go ahead and cut. Cut straight across. If you're worried about sharp corners, you can gently file them later. If you do cut your baby, press on the cut and the bleeding will quickly stop. You can also dab on antibiotic first-aid cream.

You will get better with practice—and you will get plenty of practice. Your infant's fingernails may need to be trimmed several times a week. The good news is you don't need to worry about cutting your baby's toenails. Don't worry if they look weird; they'll grow out slowly.

Early Tooth Care

Yes, you should actually start thinking about tooth-brushing now. You need to get your baby used to having her gums cleaned before her teeth come in. The first few times you try it, she's likely to bite you, and you're much better off getting those bites over with before they can draw blood. Still, it's not likely to be fun.

The best toothbrush for an infant is a gauze square (sold in the first-aid section of a drugstore) wetted with plain water. It's amazing how much gunk this can remove. My toddler's teeth were looking pretty crummy recently, with what looked to me like a thick layer of tartar. He wasn't letting me get a toothbrush near his mouth, but he did open his mouth for my dentist, who whisked that tartar off with her piece of gauze.

Mommy Must

Babies love to imitate. Try brushing your teeth in front of your baby before you try to brush his teeth. Another trick is to pretend you're looking for something silly behind your baby's teeth.

An alternative is a fingertip brush—a brush with rubber bristles that sits like a cap over your finger. You can also go straight to a toothbrush; infant toothbrushes are very soft. The downside is that they are quickly chewed into oblivion. Hold your baby against you when you brush, facing into a mirror so you can see what you're doing. Your baby is less likely to clench his mouth shut or wriggle away than when you come at him from the front.

What you don't want to introduce at this point is toothpaste. Babies will swallow it, and swallowing excess fluoride can damage the enamel of the teeth yet to come in. That said, babies over six months of age do need a certain amount of fluoride in their diet to prevent future cavities.

Sunshine and Naked Time

A number of infant-care problems can be avoided by letting your baby lie around naked. If she can spend some of her naked time in the sun—outside, or in a patch of sun from a window—so much the better. Sunbaths help prevent diaper rash, heal the umbilical cord, and head off newborn jaundice by breaking down the bilirubin in the blood. We're not talking about going for the George Hamilton look, of course. Just five minutes of sun a day, in the early morning or late afternoon, are plenty. And make sure your baby is facing away from the sun or that her eyes are covered.

Chapter 9

Dr. Mommy: Sickness in the First Year

HE'S SICK! Do you call the doctor? Run to the emergency room? Give him medicine? Or just put him back to sleep? You're the triage nurse and you have to figure it out—which isn't easy, particularly because he's still screaming. Here are some sick baby basics.

Getting Through the First Month

You're more likely to need to call the doctor while your baby is a newborn. Symptoms that are not worrisome in an older baby can indicate real trouble during a baby's first month. Let's look at some of the most common maladies of newborns.

Jaundice

Many babies develop a yellow tinge to their skin color after birth. This is caused by increased amounts of a pigment called bilirubin, which is produced by the normal breakdown of red blood cells. Normal jaundice occurs in more than 50 percent of babies, appearing at day two or three and disappearing in a week or two; it's usually harmless.

So-called breastmilk jaundice (originally thought to be caused by an enzyme in mother's milk) looks the same, but usually appears between days four and seven and can last three to ten weeks. You may find it helpful to nurse more frequently, every one-and-a-half to two-and-a-half hours during the day and at least every four hours at night. Frequent feeding may seem counterintuitive, but it does mean frequent pooping, and that helps cleanse bilirubin from the body.

Call your doctor immediately if your jaundiced baby becomes dehydrated or feverish. Call your doctor during her regular office hours if your baby looks deep yellow or orange, has fewer than three movements a day, or still looks yellow after she is fourteen days old.

Fever

Call the doctor if your baby's temperature is over 100.4°F rectally or 99.0°F axillary (under the arm). A fever in the first two months may be a sign of a serious infection, and an infection at this age can quickly overwhelm the developing immune system. Your baby may be hospitalized and treated with antibiotics.

Diarrhea

Diarrhea in newborns can quickly lead to dehydration. While babies normally have many bowel movements a day, and they are typically runny, if it looks more like water than like mustard, it is diarrhea. If you suspect diarrhea, and your baby is pooping more often than he is eating, call the doctor.

Vomiting

Projectile vomiting (vomit that shoots out of the mouth instead of dribbling down the chin) may mean your baby has an obstruction in the valve between the stomach and small intestine. Call your doctor immediately.

Vomiting after more than three feedings in a row may cause dehydration. Call your doctor if your baby doesn't pee in eight hours. You should also call if any blood appears in the vomit, or if vomiting continues for more than twenty-four hours.

Floppiness

While a newborn doesn't have a lot of muscle control, she typically kicks and squirms and waves her arms around. If she feels floppy all over or seems to lose muscle tone, she may have an infection, so call the doctor.

Shakes

A quivery chin is cute, but if your baby seems to quiver all over, your doctor needs to find out why.

Scary Symptoms in Older Babies

If your baby is more than a month old, you don't need to be quite so quick to dial the doctor. But you should call if your baby:

- Is under six months old and has a fever higher than 101°F
- Is over six months old and has a fever higher than 103°F
- Has a fever for more than two days
- Has a fever and a stiff neck, symptoms of meningitis (Check for this by holding a toy level with his face and then moving it toward the ground. If he can't follow its path by bringing his chin down to his chest, he may have a stiff neck.)
- Is too sleepy (You may be relieved if your baby suddenly starts to sleep all day and night, but a big jump in sleepiness is not normal and may indicate an infection.)
- Cries excessively
- Vomits persistently (after every feeding within twelve hours), or if the vomit contains blood
- Seems dehydrated (If your baby seems to be peeing a lot less than usual—you're changing fewer diapers—there is a problem.)
- Has trouble breathing (the skin between her ribs may suck in with each breath), or breathes extremely rapidly (more than forty breaths a minute)
- Has persistent bluish lips or fingernails (babies can briefly turn blue from the cold or from crying)
- Has a cough that lasts longer than two weeks or has a whooping or barking cough
- Has eye inflammation or discharge
- Has a rash that covers much of his body

Other than the big stuff just listed, you'll probably be treating a lot of minor illnesses in the first year, so have the following on hand:

- Thermometers—at least one oral and one rectal
- Infant acetaminophen drops or suspension
- Infant ibuprofen drops
- Topical anesthetic (useless for teething, but may help with splinter removal)
- Vaseline
- Pedialyte
- Benadryl (an antihistamine, for allergic reactions)
- Calibrated syringes or droppers for giving medicine
- Nasal aspirator
- Saline nose drops
- Diaper rash cream
- Hydrocortisone cream
- Rubbing alcohol
- Aveeno (an oatmeal bath, soothing for many skin problems)

And don't forget, for nonprescription medicines, check the label for the correct dosage. If no information is given for your baby's age or weight, call your pediatrician's office for the correct dosage.

Figuring Out Fever Basics

"Does she have a fever?" That is one of the first questions you'll be asked whenever you call your doctor with a question about a sick baby—and it will soon be one of the first questions you'll ask yourself. Eventually, you'll learn to make a pretty accurate estimate of your child's temperature by touching your lips or cheek to her forehead but you'll still need to know some numbers.

Thermometers

Be sure you have a glass thermometer, a digital thermometer, a disposable strip thermometer, or an ear thermometer. You can take a baby's temperature rectally, under his arm (axillary), or by reading the heat off his eardrum (tympanic). You can't, however, take his temperature orally; holding the thermometer under his tongue would be uncomfortable and he might gag or choke. If you use a glass thermometer, your baby might bite off the end.

I'm a fan of digital thermometers. They cost about $5, have flexible rubber tips, and beep when they are done. I find glass thermometers hard to read and

Mindful Mommy

There are many old wives' tales about fevers to be aware of—for example, do not try to lower a fever by rubbing your baby with rubbing alcohol!

worry (probably needlessly) about breakage. Disposable strips aren't very accurate. Ear thermometers are expensive (about $60) and are not considered reliable for use in babies under six months of age, because their ear canals are so small it's hard to get accurate readings from the eardrum. Ear thermometers can be a plus for older babies because they work fast. You can increase your accuracy by taking multiple readings and using the highest one.

Taking Your Baby's Temperature

If you are using a glass thermometer to take your baby's temperature rectally, make sure you have one intended for rectal use. If you are using a digital thermometer, designate one for that purpose by marking it with an indelible "R." First, clean the thermometer by wiping with rubbing alcohol or washing with soapy water. Then make sure it is reset. To reset a glass thermometer, shake it until the mercury reads below 98.6°F; to reset a digital thermometer, turn it off and then back on.

Put a dab of petroleum jelly on the tip of the thermometer. Lay your baby stomach down on the changing table and hold her with one hand placed firmly on her back; add another dab of petroleum jelly at the opening of her anus. Then insert the thermometer tip one-half inch into her rectum (never forcing it), and hold it there between your second and third fingers, with your hand cupped over her buttocks. Wait two minutes, or, if using a digital thermometer, until it beeps. A rectal temperature of 100.4°F and up is considered a fever.

To take your baby's temperature under his arm (axillary), open up or remove his clothing. Put him in a comfortable position, lying in your arms or against your chest. Put the glass or digital thermometer or fever strip in his dry armpit and tuck his elbow against his body. Cuddle him, making sure he doesn't move his arm. Wait four minutes, or until the digital thermometer beeps its all-done signal. An axillary temperature of over 99.0°F is considered a fever.

How to Treat a Fever

If your baby has a fever, make sure she isn't dressed too warmly and that her room isn't hot. You can strip her down to her T-shirt, but keep a light blanket handy for when her temperature begins to drop.

With your doctor's permission and confirmation of the dosage, give him a fever-reducing medicine, like acetaminophen (Tylenol) or ibuprofen (Motrin). You should see the fever start to come down thirty minutes later. If it doesn't, or spikes back up again quickly, these medicines can be alternated. While doses of Tylenol are meant to be given four hours apart and Motrin six hours apart, pediatricians sometimes

Mommy Knows Best

You can also try to bring your baby's fever down by giving her a bath in a few inches of lukewarm water, using a washcloth to spread water over her, then letting her air dry.

recommend giving a dose of Motrin only two hours after giving Tylenol. Just don't give a second dose of the same medicine any sooner than prescribed.

Give your feverish baby lots to drink—she's sweating-out fluids, and dehydration can make her temperature jump.

When Not to Treat a Fever

Fevers do have a purpose—they are part of a body's defenses against illness, although the exact mechanism is unclear. They may increase the number of white blood cells (which kill viruses and destroy bacteria) or raise the amount of interferon, an antiviral substance in the blood, and thus hinder bacteria and viruses from multiplying. Fevers aren't dangerous in themselves (although they serve as a warning of problems) except at extremely high levels—above 106°F. Mustering all your forces to bring your baby's temperature down every time he gets a fever isn't necessarily a good idea and may, in fact, prolong his illness.

You'll develop your own system as you figure out the way your child's body works—and every one is different.

Mindful Mommy
You will notice that your baby's fever may climb in the afternoon from a morning low. This is normal, and doesn't mean your baby is getting sicker.

Beware of Febrile Convulsions

You should, however, be aggressive in fighting fevers in children who are susceptible to febrile convulsions. One to two percent of children, most between nine months and five years old, are susceptible to these kinds of seizures, characterized by symmetrical rhythmic convulsions, eyes rolling back in the head, and a loss of consciousness. Convulsions can last as long as ten minutes, but usually disappear in less than two minutes. Although it's less common, some susceptible children experience them every time they get a fever. The seizures usually have no permanent effects.

If your child has a seizure, turn her on her side, remove any hard objects she might slam into, and look at your watch. You need to time the seizure—your doctor will want to know its duration. If the seizure lasts longer than five minutes, call your physician or local paramedics. After five minutes, the child should get emergency care and be evaluated; but seizures of that durable are rare. If your child is prone to these seizures, you will want to administer fever-reducing medicine sooner, rather than later.

Learn How to Give Medicines

"Give him one dropperful of Tylenol," your doctor says, or, "Give her one teaspoon of antibiotic." You dutifully fill the dropper or syringe up to the correct line, put it in your baby's mouth, and squirt it in.

It immediately comes dribbling back out, at which point you madly try to shovel it back in with your finger. Giving a baby medicine is not intuitive. If you're lucky, your baby will like the taste and lap it up, but don't count on it.

I was on my second baby before I knew how to give medicine so it didn't dribble out, thanks to a pediatrician who insisted on drilling me on her favorite technique before she let me out of her office. Some may differ with this technique, and if you've got a method that works for you, by all means, stick to it. This two-person strategy worked for me.

One adult sits on the floor, leaning against a wall, with her legs straight out in front of her. Another adult lays the baby on the first adult's legs, so his head is slightly higher than his body (which happens naturally since your thighs are fatter than your ankles), and the baby's feet are pointing toward the adult's feet. The first adult then lifts the baby's arms above the baby's head; this keeps his hands from knocking the medicine away and opens up his throat. The second adult slips the dropper or syringe into the side of the baby's mouth, between his cheek and where his molars will eventually appear, squirts in just a few drops of medicine, then a few more, and then a few more until the dropper is empty. It doesn't matter if the baby's mouth is shut or if he's crying; the medicine will dribble down his throat.

The first few times we tried the reclined technique, my kids screamed and squirmed, but it worked. After that, to my amazement, at medicine time they settled down immediately as soon as they were put into position.

Distraction can help make the medicine go down, too. If you can call on another adult or sibling to wave a toy or make faces at your baby, do so. Otherwise, dangle a toy from your mouth as you use both of your hands to give the medicine.

What you don't want to do is try to hide your baby's medicine in a bottle or in food. It still won't taste great, and if your baby doesn't finish the juice or food, you'll have no idea how much medicine he consumed.

If giving your baby medicine orally is always a struggle, ask your drugstore for acetaminophen suppositories. The dosage, in milligrams, is the same as that for oral medication, but is less preferable than the oral form, because the amount that is absorbed can vary.

Eye Treatments Can Be Tough, Too

You may also someday find yourself having to give your baby eye medication, in the form of drops or ointment. You'll need to have someone hold your baby's hands so she doesn't rub away the drops imme-

Mommy Knows Best

Another method to administer medicine is the cheek pocket. Use a finger to pull out a corner of your baby's mouth to make a pocket in his cheek, and drop the medicine into the pocket a little at a time. Keep the pocket open until all the medicine has been swallowed.

diately, or wrap her in a blanket. Balancing your hand on her cheek, but being careful not to touch the dropper to the eye, aim the drops for the inside corner of her eye. Her eye does not need to be open; when she blinks, the drops will get in.

If you're administering ointment, you do not need to force his eye open. Instead, squeeze out a line of ointment along the roots of his upper eyelashes (kind of like eyeliner). Keep his hands away from his eyes until the ointment melts into them. Or, pull down his lower eyelid to make a pouch and put the drops or ointment inside the pouch. If your baby really fights the eye medication, try applying it when he is asleep.

Healthy Baby Care Tips

- Whenever you change your baby's clothes, touch your lips to her forehead. You'll get to know her normal temperature this way, and will be able to quickly assess her for fever when she's sick. Make sure to always check with a thermometer though to make sure your instincts are right!
- Bubble baths can be fun for older babies, but if your baby is a girl, you might want to make them a rare treat. Bubble baths can irritate the sensitive labial and vaginal tissues, causing itchy or painful rashes.
- Trust your instincts. If your baby's doctor dismisses your concerns but you feel something is wrong, don't back down. Insist that your baby

be examined until he is better or the cause of his symptoms is found.

- If your baby's illness includes vomiting or diarrhea, line her crib with thick bath towels—these are easier to peel off and wash than the sheets.
- Try refrigerating baby's liquid medicines—they may taste better cold.
- If he really hates the taste of a medicine, have him suck on a popsicle first, to partially numb his mouth.
- Go for a drive; a sick baby may sleep better in the car than the crib.

Your baby will get sick and you will get through it. Most of us have access to excellent health care. Use it, rely on your good sense, and know that your baby will probably be better in the morning. And don't forget, take a deep breath—you're not alone Mommy!

The Cold and Other Common Illnesses

Babies catch colds—a lot of colds—particularly if they have older siblings bringing cold viruses home from school. Until your infant is about two months old, you should try to protect her from exposure to nonfamily members who have colds. Babies this young really need their noses to breathe; they don't easily switch to mouth breathing when their noses are stuffy, and therefore can be very uncomfortable.

Most colds are mild and typically last a week to ten days. It may start out with a fever, followed by stuffiness, sneezing, and, sometimes, a cough. Don't try to guard your baby against catching colds forever or try to protect him from his siblings' colds. The former will make you crazy and the latter is impossible. Unpleasant as they can be, your baby needs to have a few colds in his first year. Exposure means that he will be less susceptible to cold viruses later on, when missing a few weeks of school may set him back. It turns out that exposure to germs during their first year of life helps make a child's immune system function correctly. A recent study funded by the National Heart, Lung, and Blood Institute concluded that frequent exposure to other children (and their germs), particularly in the first six months of life, reduces the chance of a child developing asthma later on.

You shouldn't give a baby under six months any cold medications; they really don't work in babies that young and instead of helping your baby sleep better, they may make her hyperactive. Try placing a warm washcloth across her sinus area for a few minutes. Use a nasal aspirator to clear out her nose before feeding her or whenever she seems particularly uncomfortable. If you need to give your baby medication by using a nasal aspirator, hold your baby in a sitting position. Tilt her head back, put in a few drops of saline solution, and wait a minute. Then, with her head upright, squeeze the bulb of the aspirator and place just the tip into one nostril. Slowly let go of the bulb. Remove it from your baby's nose and squirt any mucus out onto a tissue. Repeat for the other nostril.

You can also temporarily clear your baby's congestion with a few drops of saline solution placed in each nostril (wait a minute or two, and then use the aspirator). Saline solution is sold in special applicators for this purpose, or you can use any commercial saline solution and a standard eyedropper. You can also make your own with one-quarter teaspoon of table salt in eight ounces of warm tap water; make up a fresh batch every day or two and store it in a clean bottle.

At night, use a vaporizer or humidifier in your baby's room to keep the nasal secretions from drying out. Elevate the head of your baby's crib by putting a pillow under the mattress or blocks under the legs of the crib. (Don't put a pillow in the crib.)

Make sure your baby drinks plenty of liquids. If you are nursing, nurse frequently. If your baby is on solid foods, offer a variety of liquids. A baby with a stuffy nose may prefer to drink from a cup since it's easier than from a bottle. You do not have to cut back on milk. Milk rarely increases the produc-

Mindful Mommy

Some women believe that you can squirt a little breast-milk in your baby's nostrils (or express it, and administer it with a dropper) to act as a decongestant. It may have the same decongestant effect as saline, and may help fight infection. If his nose and lips are getting irritated, then dab them with petroleum jelly.

tion of mucus, and any liquids your baby will drink are beneficial.

If a cough is making your baby uncomfortable, you can give him an expectorant that thins the secretions. A mild dextromethorphan-based cough suppressant may help you both sleep better at night.

While a cold itself will clear up on its own, colds can lead to secondary conditions such as ear infections, pneumonia, or bronchitis. If your baby doesn't seem to be getting better, or spikes a fever after recovering from her initial bout with fever, you may suspect a secondary infection and should call your doctor.

Vomiting and Diarrhea

In babies, vomiting and diarrhea are usually caused by viruses. Wash your hands often; viral diarrhea is very contagious. If vomiting and diarrhea continue after several feedings, your baby risks dehydration.

If you are breastfeeding and your baby has diarrhea, nurse more frequently. If you are formula-feeding, switch to Pedialyte, Rehydralyte, or a comparable nonprescription oral rehydration fluid, which will replenish electrolytes in addition to lost fluids. These rehydration fluids come plain or flavored and are available without a prescription. Stick to the plain; most babies find the flavored versions unpalatable. You can also try freezing it in popsicle form. Don't use sports drinks; they don't contain enough sodium.

Try to get your baby to drink four ounces of the solution every time he has a watery movement.

Switch back to formula if the diarrhea becomes less watery and your baby is peeing regularly. Some moms have had success treating diarrhea with barley or rice water. Cook rice or barley until very soft, then strain out the grain and put the remaining liquid in a bottle, adding one-quarter teaspoon salt to every two cups of water.

If your baby seems listless, is urinating a lot less than usual, cries with few tears, has a sunken fontanel (soft spot), or the diarrhea lasts longer than a week, call your doctor.

If your baby is vomiting, spread towels over vulnerable surfaces. Reduce nursing time, but not frequency, with your breastfed baby. If she vomits once or twice, nurse on only one side every hour or two; if she vomits more than twice, nurse for five minutes every half-hour to an hour. Return to your regular feeding pattern after eight hours without vomiting. For a formula-fed baby, switch to one of the rehydration fluids and give a teaspoonful of fluid every ten minutes, increasing the amount after four vomit-free hours. Resume normal feeding after eight hours (at which point you can start dealing with the piles of laundry).

Chamomile, peppermint, or ginger can help nausea. You can buy chamomile and peppermint in tea bags or purchase the dried herbs loose and use a tea ball; for ginger, make sure it's fresh and boil a few slices in water. These herbal remedies would be in addition to rehydration fluid for a severely vomiting baby. If the baby has just thrown up once, you could give him a few ounces in a bottle. Keep in mind that these alternatives are more appropriate for babies over six months old, and are not recommended for a baby who has never had anything but breastmilk.

Again, contact a physician if:

- There are signs of dehydration, such as no urine in eight to twelve hours
- Any blood appears in the vomit
- There seems to be abdominal pain that lasts for more than four hours
- The vomiting continues for more than twenty-four hours
- Your baby just seems really, really sick

Ear Infections

Unlike stomach viruses, which announce themselves clearly (and messily), ear infections are harder to identify, at least until your child is old enough to say "Hurts" as she points to her ear. She may pull on her ear or bat at it—but some babies do that anyway. She will probably be cranky, particularly when you try to lay her down, and may have trouble sleeping—but some babies are like that anyway. And she may eventually get a fever.

Your baby may have an ear infection if he is pulling at his ear, fussing more than usual, or seems uncomfortable when reclining (particularly if he exhibits any of these symptoms after a few days of a runny nose). Your doctor will look in your baby's ear and, if the ear is infected, will see a red ear drum that is bulging with the pressure of trapped fluid. If your doctor decides to prescribe antibiotics, the good news is that you'll see a change in your baby's behavior within forty-eight hours. If the doctor wants to wait a day or two because signs of infection are minimal, don't push for unnecessary antibiotics.

To make your baby more comfortable in the meantime, give her acetaminophen or ibuprofen to dull the pain and soothe her ear with hot compresses. Wet a washcloth with warm tap water, wring it out, and hold it over the ear (or use a heating pad), and keep her in a sitting position. Bring in her car seat and let her sleep in that or in the stroller. Pile pillows or books under the head end of the mattress if she's in her crib; lying horizontally increases the pressure on the ear. Ask your doctor to prescribe anesthetic ear drops to numb the pain.

Some babies get ear infections constantly—whenever, it seems, they get a cold. This can be more than a nuisance; an ear infection may muffle your baby's hearing just when he is learning to speak. Children do outgrow ear infections as their Eustachian tubes enlarge and change position, which improves drainage.

In the meantime, if your baby falls into this pattern, you can ask your doctor to prescribe prophylactic

Mommy Knows Best

A vaccine called Prevnar (or PCV, for pneumoccal conjugate vaccine), intended for prevention of bacterial meningitis, blood infections, and pneumonia, protects against some ear infections as well. This vaccine is universally recommended by the Centers for Disease Control and Prevention and the AAP for children in their first year.

antibiotics. These are low-dose antibiotics given every day during the worst of the cold season or for seven days every time your baby gets a cold. In general, you should avoid giving your child unnecessary antibiotics, but if she is prone to infection, this has been a proven deterrent.

Chronic ear infections can also be treated by a tympanostomy (insertion of drainage tubes in the eardrums) or the removal of tonsils or adenoids. Both procedures are performed under anesthesia, but at much lower levels than what's required for general surgery. A laser treatment that puts a hole in the eardrum for drainage and can be performed with just a topical anesthetic has been approved, but isn't in wide use.

The Truth about Croup

Croup is one of the scarier viruses. It seems to come on suddenly, usually in the middle of the night. You'll know croup when you hear it—your baby will sound like a seal barking. Croup usually lasts for five to six days, with the worst symptoms at night. Use a humidifier in the bedroom or hang wet towels up; dry air makes croup worse.

In severe cases, you may hear a raspy, vibrating sound when your baby inhales between coughs, and breathing becomes difficult. If this happens, take him into the bathroom and turn on the shower, full blast, as hot as it goes. The steam should ease his breathing. Try to calm him down by singing or reading a story—whatever works best. The more upset he is, the worse his croup will be. If steam immersion works, crank up a humidifier in his room, then put him back to bed, or bring a quilt into the steamy bathroom and lie down with him on the floor. You can also take him outside—cool, damp air can help his breathing, and the change of scene may calm him down.

If these efforts have no effect after twenty minutes, or she is struggling to breathe even when she isn't coughing or can't cry because she can't get enough breath, call your doctor immediately.

Asthma

Asthma is another scary one. Asthma can be triggered by allergies or by a virus that inflames the lining of the bronchioles. Again, the attacks usually come on at night, but can occur anytime. The child wakes up and has trouble exhaling; he panics. You may hear wheezing as your baby exhales, or notice the center of his chest, between his breastbones, pull inward when he takes a breath. Call your doctor if the breathing problems seem severe, if he's breathing rapidly (more than forty breaths a minute), or if his lips or fingertips turn blue. While you're talking to the doctor, sit your baby up and try to calm him down; crying only makes his struggles to breathe worse.

The Real Deal on Infectious Rashes

A number of infectious diseases are accompanied by a characteristic—and often uncomfortable—rash. The good news is you probably won't have to take care of a child in itchy distress from measles, rubella, or chickenpox, since your child will be vaccinated against those diseases when she turns one. As long as you breastfeed, and until about four months of age if you're bottle-feeding, your antibodies will provide some protection.

Your child is likely to come down with one of the rash-causing diseases you probably haven't heard of yet, such as coxsackie, roseola, and fifth disease.

What Is Coxsackie?

In coxsackie, also called hand, foot, and mouth disease, spots appear inside the mouth and on hands, feet, and butt. It usually comes with a fever, but the condition rarely causes long-term complications. Your baby will probably be miserable, as the mouth spots often blister, making swallowing uncomfortable. Keep nursing your younger baby; you can give an older baby juice popsicles to help soothe his throat. He might be happier drinking from a cup than a bottle, and for older babies, you can try putting half a teaspoon of a liquid antacid in front of his mouth after meals. A coxsackie bout can last as long as a week—and it makes for a very long week.

Coxsackie is very contagious from about two days before the rash appears until about two days after, with a three to six day incubation period. Because it's hard to prevent spreading this one and it is generally harmless, pediatricians don't advise making yourself crazy quarantining your child.

Explaining Roseola

The first symptom of roseola that you'll notice will be a very high fever, as high as 105°F. The fever lasts for three to four days, and there are rarely any other symptoms, so you may have no idea what is wrong. Then the fever will go away and faint pink spots appear on your baby's trunk, neck, and arms. This is good news—unlike the other rash diseases, the spots signify the end, not the beginning, of the virus. It is contagious until the rash is gone; the incubation period is about twelve days. There are no complications with roseola.

The Facts about Fifth Disease

In Fifth Disease, also called slapped-cheek disease, your baby's face will be bright red, as if her cheeks were sunburned. The rash travels to the arms and legs, then on to other parts of the body. It usually lasts for a few days, but may go on for weeks, reappearing whenever she gets warmer than usual, when taking a bath, for example. Again, this is a fairly benign virus, and causes complications only in pregnant women.

You should keep your baby away from pregnant women. However, this can be tricky. Fifth disease is mainly contagious for a week before the rash appears. Once the rash appears, your baby is no longer considered contagious. If you believe a pregnant woman has been exposed to your baby, tell her to see her OB. The OB will order an antibody test to determine if the mother was previously protected from the disease or not. If she wasn't, the pregnancy will be monitored closely. Fifth disease doesn't cause birth defects, but some infected fetuses develop severe anemia, and a small percentage die.

Other Rashes

Babies also typically get blotchy, red pimples in their second or third week. This baby acne is normal and goes away on its own. Heat can also cause a rash, particularly around your baby's neck, armpits, or diaper area. Be sure not to overdress him when the weather is hot and humid. To soothe heat-induced rashes, give your baby a cool bath every few hours, letting his skin air dry. Or, for small areas, lay a cool, damp washcloth over the area for ten minutes or so at a time.

Minor Ailments You Should Be Aware Of

The following are more of a nuisance than a crisis, but can cause problems if not treated:

- **Blocked tear duct.** A baby with a blocked tear duct (the little opening at the inside corner of the eye) looks like she is continually crying. Your baby's doctor will show you how to massage the area to open the duct. If this doesn't work after many weeks, the doctor may suggest having an ophthalmologist open the tear duct.

- **Pinkeye.** Babies with conjunctivitis, or pink-eye, have yellow discharge along with red, irritated-looking eyes. Call your doctor for antibiotic drops or ointment. You can apply cold compresses to soothe the eyes and reduce swelling. Pinkeye is highly contagious, so wash your hands frequently and thoroughly to avoid giving it to yourself or siblings.
- **Eczema.** These dry, red, and extremely itchy patches most commonly appear in the creases of the elbows, wrists, and knees, but can appear anywhere on the body. Eczema simply comes with sensitive skin, which is inherited, and flares up when the skin is irritated or from food allergies. If your baby gets eczema, use soap infrequently and detergent sparingly. Avoid wool clothing, moisturize him frequently, and when he's going through a severe bout, dab a prescription steroid cream on the scaly patches.
- **Eye infection.** If not kept open, as discussed, blocked tear ducts can turn into eye infections. Sometimes, of course, eye infections can appear out of nowhere. You'll see a watery discharge that clumps in your baby's eyelashes and sometimes seems to glue her eye shut. First, clean the eye—dip a cotton ball in clean water and wipe the eye from the inside corner to the outside. Repeat until the eye is clean, using a fresh cotton ball for each swipe.

Chapter 10

Making Time for Play Time

FOR THE FIRST FEW weeks of his life, your baby will mostly eat, sleep, and use an incredible number of diapers. Then, after he's a few weeks old, you may find that he's not tired, hungry, or wet, but he's still fussing. Why? Simply because he's bored.

The Importance of Play

Once your baby tells you she's bored, it's time to introduce her to the concept of playtime. Okay, she's only a month old, and she doesn't seem to be able to do much of anything; work with what she's got—hearing, sight, a sense of touch, a sense of smell, and some muscle control. Play that appeals to these abilities will entertain your baby and enable her to develop her mind and body.

Play is actually necessary for development. Play with others gives babies a chance to connect with them. Play with objects gives babies a chance to discover that they are powerful and that they can act on their environments. Solo play gives babies a chance to connect with themselves, and it will give you a few minutes while your baby happily entertains himself.

I wasn't that great at letting my first son, Alexander, entertain himself. He'd do about five minutes in his bouncy chair while I folded laundry next to him, but that was about as much of a break as I could get. I figured I couldn't expect much more. Then I visited a neighbor with a baby the same age—and she served me scones she had just finished baking. Her two-month-old baby hadn't taken an early nap. Rather, she had her house set up with play stations—an infant swing positioned to look outside; a baby chair on the counter with a view of the kitchen; a quilt on the floor with a few toys scattered on it. She moved her baby from station to station and this way could keep him happy and amused for as much as an hour.

Stocking the Toy Box

You don't need a lot of store-bought, primary-colored plastic objects to entertain your baby. Some of the best baby toys are things you already have around the house.

Once your baby can sit, she'll love playing with containers. Plastic food-storage containers work just as well as primary colored ones sold in toy stores. She'll play with them empty, but will like them even better with something to dump out of them—water, sand, oatmeal, and birdseed all have great dumping potential.

He'll want your television remote control. He sees other people in the family jockeying for its possession—he'll know it's important. He won't be placated with a toy one, with its chunky buttons and bright colors. Dig up an old remote (you know you have one somewhere), remove the batteries, and tape the battery cover on.

When you do buy toys, stick to the classics. Some baby toys you remember from your childhood are still around—there's a reason for that. These toys typically can be played with in a variety of ways and will interest your baby for years.

The Basics

You'll need a rattle. Even a very young baby, who instinctively grasps anything put into her hand, can wave a rattle. After you've used it yourself to teach her to follow sounds, it will be a great entertainer during diaper changes.

You'll want nesting cups that fit inside each other. This will be your baby's first puzzle. These cups can also stack, pour, be sorted into colors, and be counted.

Mommy Knows Best

Your baby will like to empty your kitchen cabinets. Don't childproof everything. Instead, make sure one or more drawers or cabinets are filled with things she can safely empty out.

They let him experiment with the ideas of inside and outside, and bigger and smaller.

You'll want stacking toys—plastic or wooden rings that stack up on a post. And you'll need lots of blocks—for touching, tasting, and banging together. Eventually, they might even be used for stacking.

You'll probably also want a toy that does something when a button or lever is pushed (a train spins around, a funny man pops up). These break the classic rule about toy flexibility, but they teach cause and effect, and babies love them. A light switch fits into this category, but just how long do you want to hold your baby up so she can turn the overhead light on and off?

You will also, particularly toward the end of the first year, need toys that let your baby imitate your activities—bowls, spoons (if you don't want to sacrifice your own), a little stove, a toy telephone, dolls, a mop, a toddler-sized stroller or shopping cart.

What you don't need are "educational" toys designed to turn your baby into a child genius. Your baby has a huge curriculum he's covering in his first year as it is. Your job is to simply expose him to life, not drill him in his numbers. Sometimes it is hard to resist,

Mommy Must

Avoid empty film containers. While babies love them—they are the perfect size for a baby to clutch and can be filled with interesting things to dump or shake—film containers absorb chemicals from film that your child should not be ingesting.

so go ahead and teach, but he'll be better off learning his academics at a more developmentally appropriate time. Brain growth, recent research shows, does not stop in early childhood as used to be thought; it continues throughout life, so really, there is no rush.

Toys You Already Have

Look around the house; you are well stocked with infant toys, you just may not realize it yet. Babies like things that go inside other things, things with lids to open and close, and things that can be stacked or dumped. They like things with interesting textures or ones that make interesting sounds. Some of the best are:

- **From the kitchen:** Wooden spoons, measuring cups and spoons, pots and pans, plastic containers with lids, balls of waxed paper or aluminum foil (bigger than your baby's fist)
- **From the bathroom:** Clean makeup brushes, cloth diapers, empty tissue box filled with light scarves, empty baby wipe container, nylon net bath puff
- **Just stuff:** Coasters, napkin rings, socks rolled into balls or used as puppets, clean feather duster, shoes, old wallets and credit cards
- **Filled clear plastic bottles:** Clear or colored water, liquid soap, dry pasta, feathers, rice, or anything else that fits, makes noise, and looks fun (glue or tape the top on to prevent choking hazards and messes)

To be safe, be sure your baby's playthings meet these criteria:

- The paint is nontoxic
- It has no small detachable parts
- None of the edges or corners are sharp
- No bells and whistles are at excessive decibels (some toy trucks emit siren noises that rival those from real fire trucks)
- No "bean-bag" stuffing (the pellets that stuff them are a choking hazard, so stick to cuddlers stuffed with fluff)
- The toy doesn't have long or loose cords, strings, or ribbons (avoid anything, including necklaces, that your baby can get tangled around herself)
- The toy, and any detachable parts, are too large to fit inside a toilet-paper tube

Encourage Development with Games

Use playtime to encourage development by providing lots of opportunity for practice. Get him out of his infant seat and onto the floor, give him interesting objects to look at and reach for, take him out into the world and tell him about the world he's seeing. Use baby games that combine several of the senses and teach important lessons.

Everybody likes to play peek-a-boo with a baby—probably because it gets such a great reaction. Cover your face with a baby blanket or burp cloth and whisk the cloth away, saying "Peek-a-boo!" You can also cover a toy with the blanket and then make it reappear with a flourish. Or cover your baby's head and let her pull off the blanket and say peek-a-boo to you. This teaches object permanence—that when things are gone, they aren't gone forever.

Lay your month-old baby down in the middle of the floor and move around the room, talking to him. As he hunts for the source of the sound of your voice, he starts to associate sights and sounds. Once your baby is crawling, partially hide behind a couch or doorway and call him to find you. When he gets good at this game, hide completely, but still call out. Eventually, your baby will be able to hunt you down without the help of your voice. This also teaches object permanence—when mom is gone, she will come back.

Sit down and put your baby on your knees, facing you, or straddling your ankles, lying forward against your legs. Support her firmly under the arms as you bounce her gently (she shouldn't pop off of your leg) to the rhythm of a favorite rhyme. This teaches her balance, rhythm, and anticipation as she hears the

Mindful Mommy

Watch out for coins as playthings. Your baby may love to dump out your change, but coins are a big choking hazard.

same rhyme over and over and learns to expect her favorite part ("had a great fall").

Keep in mind that unless his muscles, brain, and nervous system have matured to the required level, no amount of practice will get him to a milestone before he's ready. Don't make yourself—or your baby—crazy by trying to push him to achieve every milestone as soon as possible.

Quality Time with Fellow Babies

Child development may be most visible when it comes to physical growth and mobility, but along with strengthening muscles and improving coordination, your baby is developing in other ways. She's figuring out her feelings about her world and about other people. Your baby needs friends her own age to encourage that exploration. Although she may not be old enough to do more than lie on a blanket and kick her legs, getting her together regularly with other babies who are lying and kicking is important.

Playmates

Researchers used to think young babies didn't really interact, and all two year olds did was parallel play (sit near and imitate each other, but not really play together).

My kids' behavior didn't fit in with this theory. They made close friendships before they could talk (they'd wriggle like crazy when they saw a friend in the park), and their friends' names were among the first words they said. And it is pretty hard for me to define the wild game of hide and seek that Mischa and his friend Karly have been doing since they could crawl—thundering from room to room, accompanied by shrieks and giggles—as merely parallel play.

Research has caught up with what a lot of parents know from observations: Peer relationships start early and are different from parental or sibling relationships. At two months, those two babies on a blanket will probably just look at each other; at three months, they may try to touch each other; at seven or eight months, one may crawl over to the other (or over the other) and try to hand him a toy. In fact, for a while you'll think your child is wonderful at sharing, as he's trying to give toys to everyone (the "No, mine!" stage comes later).

Playgroups

If you do need encouragement to start socializing, there are two things to keep in mind. You'll stay a lot saner if you spend some time with moms of children the same age, and long-term studies have shown that children who form good friendships early do better in school later on.

Start a playgroup. Find out if there is a mothers' club in your area—most mothers' clubs sponsor playgroups. Attend a parenting class sponsored by your local hospital—"graduates" of some of these classes form playgroups. Take a lot of walks, get the phone numbers of other baby-toting mothers that you meet, and organize your own.

Try to start out with at least five or six other parents—that way, if one or two miss a session, you'll still have a good number of members. Schedule your meetings at least weekly (you'll probably find that early morning hours are best for infants, but you'll shift the time as the babies get older and nap schedules evolve). While many playgroups successfully meet at parks, sometimes kids—and moms—interact best at playgroups hosted at the members' houses. The group is less easily scattered, and your baby will get the idea of sharing her toys before she even knows that they are her toys.

Social Milestones

As a newborn, your baby will be able to recognize his parents' voices and the voices of other people that surrounded his mother during pregnancy—siblings (if he has them), the cast of his mother's favorite television show. He will also be sensitive to the

Mommy Must

If you want to form your own playgroup, ask your pediatrician to recommend other mothers, or post a sign in her office with all the details.

feelings of others, particularly his mother. He'll notice if mom's feeling tense and will quickly become tense himself.

By four to eight weeks, your baby will probably be actively smiling in response to things that make her happy—like hearing her mother's voice. Around the age of two months, she will probably turn her head in the direction of a parent's voice and spend many happy moments gazing directly into your eyes.

When your baby is around four months old, you'll hear his first laugh and will put yourself through all sorts of crazy antics trying to get him to repeat it. Also around four months, you'll be able to tell when he's excited—he'll squeal, wriggle, or breathe heavily.

At around six months, another emotion will emerge—anger. You'll discover that your baby's angry cry is much different from her tired or hungry cry. This one won't be as much fun for you as joy and excitement, but it's an important one for your baby, because anger is motivating. A child who is mad that her favorite toy has rolled out of reach is motivated to wriggle over to it, developing her motor skills. Around the same time, your baby will also begin to recognize the difference between an angry voice and a friendly voice, and react accordingly.

Separation Anxiety:
Get Help with a Lovey

Separation anxiety usually strikes at around eight months. It starts when your baby first falls deeply in love with his primary caregiver, the person most often feeding and cuddling him. This person will be showered with adoring looks and joyous greetings and tortured by the baby's misery whenever he or she is out of sight.

Like most other species, human babies develop this passionate attachment just before they are about to move independently. (Want a duckling to follow you everywhere? Adopt it just as it's about to waddle.) Your baby realizes that she can be independent from you and is therefore afraid that you'll move away from her. And, frustrating as it can be, separation anxiety is a plus—it makes it less likely that your newly mobile baby will be moving herself out of your sight.

The best way of dealing with separation anxiety is to simply go along with it. If your baby is clingy, let him cling, or pick him up and cuddle him; if he wants to explore, smile and nod at his explorations from across the room. If he doesn't want to leave you,

Mommy Knows Best

Stranger and separation anxiety are normal results of your baby's growing independence and self-awareness. Be patient and understanding as these phases come and go.

pick him up and move him from room to room as you go.

Once she's moving on her own, move slowly so she can catch up with you. In a couple of weeks, her speed will have picked up, she'll be more confident of her ability to follow you, and, therefore, less panicked when you move. Or keep up a constant conversation if you step out of the room; if she can hear your voice, she may not be so worried. You can play hide-and-seek (peek out from your hiding place and call her) to get her used to you appearing and disappearing.

A lovey—a special blanket or toy—might help you and your baby through this phase. The lovey will remind your baby of you when you're not around.

Chapter 11

Chatting with Your Baby

YOU'VE BEEN COMMUNICATING WITH your baby since you found out you were pregnant. Now that he's here in the world with you, don't stop talking! The sound of your voice will comfort him as a newborn and guide him as he grows. Reading, signing, and telling stories to your baby are critical for language development.

Setting the Example

In your baby's first year, her senses and muscles are programmed for quick development, but they can't develop without stimulation. In a famous experiment, kittens were blindfolded at birth. Some time later, the blindfolds were removed. The kittens, who had physically normal eyes, were never able to see, because their vision was not stimulated during a developmentally critical period.

Of your baby's senses, the sense of hearing is most developed at birth. He began listening before he was born. He's used to the sound of your voice and he likes it—a lot. So talk to him. You'll find that you'll naturally raise the pitch of your voice and talk in a sing-song pattern—these are the sounds he wants to hear, and you automatically know how to make them.

You won't, however, necessarily know what to say. In fact, you might feel pretty silly talking to someone who doesn't talk back; but you'll get used to it. You shouldn't talk baby talk. You're better off saying "blanket" than "bankie," for example, to allow your baby to hear all of the sounds of the language she will soon be speaking. You do, however, need to forget about pronouns for a while. Instead of "I," "you," and "he," say "Mama," "Susie," and "Daddy." Right now, Susie's finding out that everything has a name; later she'll figure out that lots of people can be called "she" or "you."

Pretend you're the narrator of a show starring your baby. Whatever you're doing, describe it. "Mama is taking off Susie's pajamas. One snap, two snaps, three snaps, four snaps. Oh! There's Susie's tummy. Mama gives Susie's tummy a kiss. Kiss! Now Susie needs a new diaper. Okay, here's the diaper now."

If your baby responds with any kind of noise, act like she's talking back. Pause to let her finish her comment, and then respond. You can have great conversations, and, for now, your baby will agree with anything you say. Savor this!

How Your Baby Communicates

A newborn communicates through crying, which will quickly turn into a vocabulary. If you've been listening attentively, you will probably be able to distinguish cries of pain, hunger, and exhaustion. At around a month, you may find your baby imitating you by opening and closing her mouth when you speak.

Around six weeks or so, you'll begin to hear classic baby coos. These are strings of vowel sounds, like "aahh," "eeeh," and "uhh."

Language Milestones	
Age	Milestone
newborn	cries
1–2 months	cries differently to communicate pain, hunger, and exhaustion
6 weeks–2 months	coos or oohs (vowels)
4–5 months	understands his name
4–8 months	babbles (consonants)
9 months	understands "no"
10–12 months	babbles without repeating syllables
8–14 months	points
10 months	responds to a spoken request
10–18 months	says first words

Somewhere between four and eight months, your baby will add consonants, like "gagaga" and "dadada." Since the most common first consonants are "g," "k," "l," and "d," he won't, however, be saying "mama" yet, unfair as that may seem. By ten months or so, he'll progress from repeating the same syllable to babbling strings of different syllables in a cadence that sounds a lot like talking.

Meanwhile, she's learned to understand her name, the word "no," and a few other simple words. Between ten and twelve months, she will respond to a simple, spoken request such as "wave bye-bye" or "give me the ball." Enjoy this phase; in about another year she'll quite gleefully do the opposite of what you ask.

Between eight and fourteen months, he'll begin to point. That's a recognizable attempt at sign language, and, if you're interested in signing with your baby, a signal that he's ready to learn more signs (see page 184).

Sometime between nine and eighteen months, she'll say her first words.

Rhymes and Rhythm

Sometimes, you'll feel like you've completely run out of things to talk about. That's why we have nursery rhymes. Babies love the rhythm of rhymes. They also

Mindful Mommy

As many as 4 in 1,000 infants have some form of irreversible hearing impairment. The earlier it is addressed, the more likely the child is to develop language normally. A simple test that measures brain activity in response to tone and sound is available. Ask for one before you take your newborn home from the hospital.

like hearing the same rhyme over and over again, and come to anticipate what you'll say next. So you don't need to know a lot of them; a few basic ones are sufficient. You can also get a Mother Goose book out of the library and learn a few of the more obscure rhymes, just for fun. Here's a refresher on those old nursery rhymes.

Basic Rhymes

Jack and Jill
Went up the hill
To fetch a pail of water.
Jack fell down
And broke his crown
And Jill came tumbling after.

Rub-a-dub-dub
Three men in a tub
And who do you think they be?
The butcher, the baker, the candlestick maker
They all jumped out of a rotten potato
Turn 'em out, knaves all three!

Little Miss Muffet
Sat on a tuffet
Eating her curds and whey.
Along came a spider
Who sat down beside her
And frightened Miss Muffet away.

Hey diddle diddle
The cat and the fiddle
The cow jumped over the moon.
The little dog laughed
To see such sport
And the dish ran away with the spoon.

Bouncing and Movement Rhymes

To market, to market, to buy a fat pig
Home again, home again, jiggety-jig.
To market, to market, to buy a fat hog
Home again, home again, jiggety-jog.

Humpty Dumpty sat on a wall
Humpty Dumpty had a great fall
All the king's horses and all the king's men
Couldn't put Humpty together again.

Row, row, row, your boat
Gently down the stream.
Merrily, merrily, merrily, merrily
Life is but a dream.

Finger (or Toe) Play Rhymes

These are baby's fingers (touch fingers)
These are baby's toes (touch toes)
This is baby's bellybutton (touch bellybutton)
Round and round it goes (draw circles on belly)

This little piggy went to market
This little piggy stayed home
This little piggy had roast beef
This little piggy had none
And this little piggy went wee-wee-wee-wee
All the way home

Pat-a-cake, pat-a-cake
Baker's man
Bake me a cake!
As fast as you can
Roll it, and fold it,
and mark it with a B,
And put it in the oven
for Baby and me.

Here sits the Lord Mayor (touch forehead)
Here sits his two men (touch eyebrows)
Here sit the ladies (touch cheeks)
And here sits the hen (touch nose)
Here sit the little chickens (touch chin)
And here they run in (touch mouth).

Head and shoulders, knees and toes, knees
   and toes.
Head and shoulders, knees and toes, knees
   and toes.
Eyes and ears and mouth and nose.
Head and shoulders, knees and toes, knees
   and toes.

Baby Sign Language Basics

Introduce basic sign language as early as you'd like; your baby may be signing as early as nine months. When my second child was seven or eight months old, I taught her a few simple signs at dinnertime, when she was sitting in her highchair and her hands were free. She learned them quickly and continued to use the sign for "more" long after she was also saying the word. (Despite my intentions, I didn't sign with my third child—it seemed I never had a free hand when I was with him.)

Research has demonstrated that early use of sign language may encourage the development of spoken language. But the big bonus of a baby who signs is the potential reduction in frustration—and accompanying tantrums—because he can tell you what is bothering him.

Exactly what sign you use for a particular word isn't important, as long as you are consistent. You can make up your own, get a book of simple signs intended to be used with babies, use American Sign Language standard signage (animated tutorials are

Mommy Knows Best

Worried because your baby is slow to talk? Babies can't do everything at once. Some babies focus on motor skills first, and may get around to working on language later than a more sedentary baby. As long as she's hearing language, your baby is learning to talk, whether she demonstrates it at nine months or eighteen months.

easy to find on the web, and a host of books are also available), or use a mixture of all three.

Story Time

You should also read aloud. Read from baby books or from whatever magazine or newspaper you'd like. When reading to your baby, remember that you're reading, seeing, and interpreting for two. This is your best opportunity to provide editorial commentary!

Discuss the story as you go, pointing out pictures that relate directly to the story or to familiar things. "See the cat? That's just like Grandma's cat!" Ask questions about how or why things are happening in the story and speculate as to what the answers might be. Really, just verbalize your own observations and processing.

Read the same book over and over if that's what your child wants. Even if you're bored and ready to move on—he's not. On the most basic levels, repetition develops memory and comprehension.

Finally, improvise. Your baby's favorite part may be something that you add. This could be your big chance to explore your wild theatrical or literary side.

Lullabies, Reggae, Jazz, and More

Babies love music, so no matter how poorly you do it, sing—you will have an appreciative audience. Turn on the stereo to music you like. Your baby will probably like it too, whether it's rock or reggae or classical. You don't need to buy special tapes of baby music (unless you have a particular fondness for the sounds of Sesame Street or the Barney song). Down the road, you'll be listening to your kid's favorite music often enough; now's your chance to get her to listen to your favorites.

If you have a wind-up music box (on a mobile, in a stuffed animal, or freestanding), you'll use it a lot. Now to entertain your baby in the crib or on the changing table, and later when your baby figures out how to wind it up himself.

You'll also be using musical instruments for a long time. Your baby's first instrument will be a rattle. Initially, you'll shake it for her. Try shaking it on one side of her head, and then the other. After a while, she'll start looking around, trying to figure out what is making the sound. At about four months, she'll be ready to hold the rattle for herself. At six months or so, she'll start banging rattles together to hear the different sounds that makes. At this point, she'll be ready for more complex musical instruments, like drums or tambourines.

Besides music, introduce your baby to animal sounds. If you hear a bird or a dog outside, imitate it. If you look at a book about animals, make all the sounds.

Intellectual Milestones

Even though babies aren't quite ready to fill out I.Q. tests, researchers still know quite a bit about what is going on in their minds. Babies start to recognize their mothers' faces between one and two months.

At two months or so, they become interested in things beside themselves and their mothers—this is the time to get out the toys. This is a useful development, because it means your baby can be distracted when he is fussy.

Between the ages of three and four months, your baby can understand that three objects are more than two. At around four months, she learns to anticipate regular events. For example, she may open her mouth when she sees you getting out your nursing pillow or taking a bottle out of the refrigerator.

Intellectual Milestones	
Age	Milestone
1–2 months	recognizes his mother or primary caregiver
2 months	interested in things besides himself and caregiver
3 months	can discriminate between the possible (block sits on table) and the impossible (block floats in air)
3–4 months	understands that three objects are more than two
4 months	demonstrates preferences
4 months	anticipates events
5 months	follows another person's gaze
6–9 months	recognizes that his face in a mirror is a reflection
8 months	understands object permanence
8–9 months	can set a goal and ignore distraction while pursuing it

At around four months, your baby will start preferring certain people or certain toys to others. At five months or so, he'll learn to follow another person's gaze—if you look up at an airplane your baby will probably look up, too. Somewhere between six and nine months, he'll recognize that a face that he sees in a mirror is his reflection, not another baby, and may spend hours exploring that phenomenon.

At around eight months, she'll understand object permanence—that when you leave the room or a toy is hidden out of sight, it continues to exist. You can test this understanding by hiding a toy under a blanket. Until your baby understands object permanence, she won't bother to look for it, but may cry because it's gone. By eight or nine months, your baby will be able to set a goal (get a toy), make a plan to carry it out (crawl around the table), and ignore distractions (you calling her in the other direction) while she carries out her plan.

Enjoy watching your baby develop—it'll happen so fast, cherish the growth process!

Chapter 12

On the Move: Motor Development and Safety

YOUR BABY IS ONLY three days old, but clearly he's a genius. He already knows how to grab your finger and move his feet like he's walking. Well, okay, those are just reflexes. But hey, wasn't that a smile? Although babies don't smile in response to your smile until two months or so, you may catch a few smiles from a newborn.

What is "Normal," Anyway?

If this is your first child, you'll be eager to fill in that list, noting when she first rolls over, sits up, and crawls. If this is your second or third baby, you'll probably have mixed feelings when she hits a milestone. You'll be applauding her achievement, but will be aware of how much it will change your life. A baby who turns over is no longer easy to diaper; a baby who crawls needs a childproofed house. And you may be mourning the passing of an earlier stage.

First mom or experienced mom, you'll be noting your baby's developmental milestones and, whether you plan to or not, comparing them to those of your baby's peers. Odds are he'll do some things earlier than others, some things later, and once in a while will hit the median. You may be running out for safety gates months earlier than you had expected or wondering why your baby hasn't taken a step while other babies his age are jogging. He may be focused on learning to talk and will get to walking later; however he's progressing, don't forget that there is a wide range of "normal."

Vision and Touch

At birth, sight is the least developed of the senses. Babies are nearsighted, and the world is pretty much out of focus. They focus best about eight inches from their noses, and can't see much beyond eighteen inches from their nose. Babies' vision develops at different rates; your baby may have nearly normal vision by six months, or it may take years.

In the beginning, babies prefer to look at faces—particularly their mother's face—more than anything else. So give your baby plenty of face time. Hold her on your lap and gaze at her; sit her in her chair and make faces at her.

Give him other things to look at as well, factoring in that critical eight-inch distance for the first two months or so. You've probably hung a mobile over the changing table and maybe another one hangs over the crib, but babies would rather look at something new than something they've seen before, so change these mobiles regularly (simple cutout shapes or pictures from magazines are fine).

Take your baby on a flying tour. I have to credit Steve Wozniak, cofounder of Apple Computer Inc., for coming up with this idea and demonstrating it to me several years ago. You can do this as soon as your baby is strong enough to hold his head up on his own, while he's still light enough for you to carry easily on outstretched arms. Put one hand under his chest, fingers splayed wide so you can feel his muscles. Use the other hand to support his pelvis. Start near an interesting spot and hold your baby in the air. Then try to sense which way his muscles are trying to tug him. It may take you a few minutes, but you'll begin to be able to tell which way he wants to go. Resist the urge to take him to where you see him looking, let his muscles guide you instead.

Use the mirrors in your house or buy an unbreakable mirror for your baby to play with. Look in a mirror with your baby, make faces, and label your expression (happy, sad, angry). Encourage her to

Mommy Must

Go sightseeing. Carry your baby around the house, looking for things that, to a baby, would be a point of interest—a brightly colored bouquet of flowers, a shiny teakettle, or a patch of sunlight on the carpet.

touch the baby in the mirror—one day she'll figure out that it's her and be amazed. Act as a mirror for your baby; when she makes a face, you make the same face. She'll be thrilled with her power!

When your baby is a newborn, you'll be doing most of the touching. Remember that it's not just hands that can feel things; sensitivity to touch develops from the top down—your baby's face will be able to distinguish different sensations sooner than his hands will. Use a makeup brush or large paintbrush to pretend-paint your child, talking about the parts of his body as you do it. Or stroke him with a cotton ball or even a cloth diaper or blanket. You can keep a clean feather duster near your changing table and "dust" your baby when you change him. Blow gently on your baby's stomach or kiss his toes.

Self-Discovery

By two or three months, your baby will have figured out that her hands belong to her, and will watch them as she's playing with them, trying to reach out and touch objects. For a while, her hands will be her favorite toy. You can vary this game by putting a brightly colored sock or wrist rattle on one of her hands.

Mindful Mommy

Stock up on bubble soap. Bubbles move slowly, float in interesting patterns, and catch the light; they'll give your baby lots of eye-tracking practice. Later on, he'll begin to try to catch the bubbles, developing his hand-eye coordination.

Once he's figured out that he has hands, it's time for batting practice. You can buy an official cradle gym (straps over the crib), baby gym (self-supporting and can be placed over your baby when he's lying on the floor), or a bouncy chair with a toy bar, all of which he can bat at (and give you a break from being the main entertainment).

By four months or so, your baby will be tired of hitting things and will want to take them in her hands—and bring them to her mouth.

Put a toy in your hand and hold it out to your baby— then be patient. It will take him a while to calculate the path from his hand to the object. If you rush to put the toy in his hand, you'll interrupt this process.

Massage 101

Massage is a great way to relax some babies, and it is easy to do—you don't need special classes, although such classes abound.

For your baby's first few massages, just massage her arms, hands, legs, and feet (the face and chest are a lot more sensitive). Use a cold-pressed vegetable oil and warm it first by rubbing it between your palms. Avoid baby oil; it's made of petroleum and you don't want your baby sucking it off of her arm.

You don't need to know any fancy massage moves—slow, gentle stroking is really all it takes. You might start with your baby's hand, perhaps with a finger-play poem. Then rub his palm gently, starting with your thumbs in the center and moving them out along the fingers. Do both hands, and, if he approves, move on to his feet. Remember to stroke very slowly, moving down away from his head.

For her chest, start with your hands in the center, and move them away from each other, down to her sides, following the line of her rib cage. On her stomach, move your hands clockwise around her bellybutton (this is the direction the large intestine turns). Caution: Don't massage her stomach unless her umbilical cord has fallen off and there is no redness in the area. You can even do a gentle face massage, making small circles with your fingers around your baby's cheeks, stroking behind the ears, and smoothing her forehead from the center outward.

If you want a few advanced moves, try:

- **Milking**—Gently tighten your hand around his leg as you pull down toward his foot.
- **Criss-cross**—Put one hand on each of her shoulders, stroke one hand down toward her opposite hip, then repeat with the other hand. Then reverse, going back up to the shoulders.
- **Rock-a-bye**—Put your hands gently on his stomach and rock him from side to side.

Mommy Knows Best

Unlike adult massage, which calls for pushing down into the muscles, baby massage is a surface massage, using gentle and smooth strokes.

- **Bread dough**—Hold her arm between your two palms and roll it back and forth.
- **This little piggy**—Rotate each toe of your baby's foot, then gently massage the sole of the foot with your thumbs.

Dexterity Begins

At eight or nine months, your baby will begin to use his fingers and thumbs separately. This is when the pincer grasp (thumb and forefinger) develops, and he can be happily entertained for long stretches (long in baby time, anyway) trying to pick up Cheerios and put them into his mouth. At this stage, he'll begin to feel things by rubbing them between his thumb and forefinger. Make a toy for the car by securely sewing scraps of different types of fabric—silk, velvet, corduroy, lace—together.

She will also want to poke her index finger into things. A set of wooden rings, meant to be stacked on a rod, fascinated my babies at this age—they would hook their fingers through one in each hand and carry them as they crawled.

Soon after this stage, your baby will start to learn how to let go of things (I called it "testing gravity"). You'll first notice it in the high chair, as your baby deliberately drops things off the side and expects you to pick them up—again and again and again. He acts like it's a game, and it is. If you don't want him playing it with his food, give him other opportunities to practice with beanbags, balls, or blocks. Place a basket under his highchair and encourage him to drop the toys in it—it will make cleanup easier.

By nine months or so, your baby may be ready to start scribbling. Readiness for this game doesn't hinge so much on whether your baby can hold a fat crayon or chalk and use it to make marks on paper, but on whether or not she still insists on eating the crayon or chalk.

Tummy Time

Get double duty from playtime. Your baby should have plenty of opportunities to kick on his back—you can hold a beach ball over him and encourage him to kick it. In fact, the more time he has on the floor—in all positions—the better. Unlike car seats, swings, and infant carriers, when he's on the floor, he's in charge of how he moves.

Tummy time is important from the beginning. A newborn placed on her stomach will try to lift and turn her head. She'll do little pushups, and, as the months go on and her muscles develop, rock up onto

Mindful Mommy

Babies used to spend a lot of time on their stomachs, because that's the way they slept. Now babies are put to sleep on their backs—and typically don't get much tummy time.

her knees. Eventually, tummy time typically turns into crawling.

So, when your baby is awake and ready to play, you don't always need to recline him in an infant chair or lay him down on his back. The American Academy of Pediatrics recommends that babies spend some time every day on their tummies, with an adult nearby.

If you have a quilt (not a fluffy comforter, but a cotton quilt that easily lies flat), use it for tummy time. A bare floor is too hard; a carpet sheds fibers that end up being inhaled and swallowed. Lie down face to face with your baby, or put some toys in front of her to encourage her to pick up her head and look around.

Once your baby is crawling, use a bunch of couch cushions to create an obstacle course that he'll crawl around or over. Scatter a few toys around the room a short crawl from your baby. Give him things that scoot out of his reach and beg to be chased—balls or light toys on wheels. Get down on your hands and knees and let him chase you, and then chase him back.

Lift her up above your head while holding her firmly under her armpits; she'll look down at you and probably stretch out her arms and legs.

Let him jump. Hold him under his arms, and with the soles of his feet on your lap, lower him to bend his knees, and then lift him up into the air. Pretty soon, he'll bend and straighten his legs himself—and he'll be jumping, though you'll support much of his weight. When he is four months old or so, he can start jumping in a spring-loaded baby seat that hangs from a doorframe—adjust it so he can touch the floor lightly with his legs. He may just hang there the first few times you try it, but in a few days will push himself up and down.

Motor Skills Milestones

The first voluntary muscle movement a baby usually makes is turning her head. The head turn, which you'll usually see in your baby's first few weeks, develops the neck muscles and starts the progression of muscle movements that, several months down the line, will allow your baby to flip herself over.

To encourage your baby's attempt at a side-to-side head turn, lie down next to him until he looks at you. Then jump up and run around him and lie down on his other side until he looks your way again. This move is great for getting parents in shape, but if it's too much for you these days, put a toy or a mirror on one side of him and switch its position.

Mommy Must

Bicycle your baby's legs from the time he is an infant. Initially, you'll do all the work, but after a few months, he'll push against your hands as you move his feet. Eventually, you can bicycle side by side.

After the head turn comes the mini pushup, a move that takes a little bit of shoulder muscle to pull off. In the mini pushup, which your baby will probably conquer between the ages of two and four months, she will use her arms to lift her shoulders and chest (but not that big baby belly) off of the ground. For pushup practice, put her on her belly on the floor, then hold a toy in front of and slightly above her head so she needs to lift herself up for a good look.

Motor Milestones	
Age	Milestone
Birth–1 month	side to side head turn
2–4 months	mini-pushup
2–5 months	swipes at object
2–5 months	brings both hands together
3–7 months	rolls over
3–7 months	grasps objects
5–9 months	sits unsupported
6–12 months	crawls (or somehow travels on four limbs)
7–13 months	pulls up to a stand
8–17 months	walks

The Swipe and Grab

Two early motor milestones that seem simple actually require developmental prowess to achieve: the swipe and the grab. You'll usually see this between the ages of two and five months. To perform the swipe and grab, your baby needs to overcome one reflex he was born with: the tonic neck reflex. This reflex puts his arms in a fencing position—one arm extended, the other arm bent—whenever he is placed on his back with his head to one side. He can't get control of his hands until he can suppress this reflex and get both hands in front of him. Then, he needs to recognize his hands as something he can control and move toward other objects he can see.

To encourage her to swipe, use a baby gym. These are available for cribs, for floor play, and for infant seats. To encourage her to bring both hands together in a baby version of a clap, sit her in her baby chair and play patty-cake, clapping the rhyme with your own hands and then with hers.

From batting at objects, the next obvious step is grabbing them, and babies usually reach this milestone between three and five months. To voluntarily grab something, your baby needs to override the grasp reflex that makes him close his hands tightly whenever something touches his palms.

Roll Over

The roll is not only a very noticeable milestone, but for many babies is their first attempt at independent motion. You'll see it sometime between three to seven months. A baby that spends a lot of time on her stomach may roll sooner rather than later, using the front-to-back roll. This is a fairly simple movement compared to the back-to-front roll. Babies that spend most of their days on their backs will likely roll later, starting with the back-to-front roll. Once your baby masters both rolls, you may be surprised one afternoon when you put her down in the middle of the rug for a little playtime, leave the room for half a minute, and come back to find her hiding under the coffee table.

To encourage your baby to roll, make sure he gets plenty of tummy time. If he's willing, roll him across the room like a rolling pin. You can also use a pillow or rolled blanket to prop your baby on his side, lie down on his other side, and tempt him to reach for you or a toy that you're holding. If he stretches his arm out enough, he probably will topple over. The roll will impress friends and grandparents, but will make your life more difficult, since you'll no longer be able to count on your baby staying where you put him.

The Sit

The sit, which appears at an average of five to nine months, and may arrive before or after the roll, will make your life a lot easier. A sitting baby has free hands and can entertain herself by picking up and dropping toys while you entertain yourself by, oh, doing laundry or putting away dishes. (When you've had to do both with a baby on your hip for six months or so, it is a thrill to do them with both arms free.)

For sitting practice, surround him with pillows for him to keep his balance, but stay close; he'll tip over and need rescuing regularly. Or sit behind him, with him leaning back against you, and use his hands to pull him gently up into a sitting position.

Crawling, Standing, and Walking

The next big milestone for your baby, and a major life change for you, is the crawl. While a rolling baby can travel only a few yards at a time, a crawling baby can go just about anywhere—and doesn't like to be stopped.

Your baby may scoot about in a sitting position, creep or "commando crawl" (move around on her stomach, using her hands, elbows, knees, and feet for propulsion, looking like a soldier scurrying under barbed wire), or "elephant walk" (move around on all fours, but support herself on her feet instead of her knees). Not all babies do an official hand-and-knee crawl, and the fear that a failure to crawl means reading difficulties later on has been put to rest.

Your baby may skip the crawling stage altogether and focus on learning to walk upright. In fact, this is becoming more common, with an increasing number of babies going directly from sitting to walking because they spend so little time on their stomachs. There seems to be no medical consequence to this change.

Upstanding Citizen

Once your baby starts pulling himself upright, he'll be pulling up on every object in sight, even at night. Sometimes, even babies who are great sleepers have a spate of interrupted nights when, barely half-awake, they pull up in their cribs and discover they don't know how to get down. Once your baby starts pulling up, begin teaching him how to bend his knees and sit down again. Standing supported, a skill your baby will probably demonstrate between the ages of seven to thirteen months, takes the development of the muscles around his joints, general muscle strength in his legs and arms, some coordination, and a sense of balance.

To help your baby in her standing attempts, keep her barefoot as much as possible; she'll be more confident about standing if she can feel the floor. Your baby doesn't need shoes to support her feet, and they get in the way rather than help when she's starting to stand and walk. If it's cold, put her in well-fitting socks with nonskid bottoms. Thick carpeting may give her trouble (even though it reassures you about falls), so let her practice on wood or linoleum floors. Make sure she has plenty of solid, safe objects to pull up on.

Walk This Way

After standing comes walking, at ten to sixteen months. Heavy babies may fall to the late end of that spectrum; adventurous babies may walk on the early side. The level of parental protectiveness does play

Mommy Knows Best

Don't obsess about whether or not your baby is on some expert's schedule; the only schedule she's likely to be following is her own. But do be sure to applaud her every step of the way—babies thrive on enthusiastic audiences.

a role; try to reign in your fears. Early walkers may fall more often than their later-walking peers, but are unlikely to get seriously injured.

To encourage your baby to walk, simply move just out of reach, hold out your arms, and call him toward you. Some babies learn to walk by wheeling push toys around. If you think all your baby needs is a little confidence, hand him a toy when he is standing, and he may think that he is holding on to something supportive and take a step. My son Mischa took his first steps clutching a garden hose in both hands, clearly convinced that it was holding him up.

No milestone chart can tell you what your baby will—or should—be doing at a particular age. Indeed, child development experts differ in their opinions of when milestones can occur, and those opinions change. Most babies do roll over between four to six months of age. Less than ten years ago, more rolled over in the earlier part of that range than today; today's babies are sleeping on their backs and getting less practice pushing up on their arms and lifting their torsos than the stomach-sleepers of the past.

Hitting a single milestone late or early doesn't mean much in the scheme of things. It rarely indicates a problem, although falling behind normal ranges in many milestones may indicate that something is up, and you should consult with your pediatrician.

Slower development may simply be a sign of your child's personality. Some children have more cautious personalities than others; some learn by watching rather than doing. A doer may walk sooner but take a lot of spills; a watcher may walk later with hardly a wobble.

Basic Childproofing

Once your baby's on the move, you'll need to figure out how to keep her from hurting herself in her travels around the house. Before you buy a lot of child-proofing gear, do the simple things. If you don't want your books all over the floor, replace the books on the lower shelves with your baby's books, or stuff extra books in each row until they're jammed in too tight to move. Gather up any poisonous items, from detergent to vitamins, and put them on your highest shelves (locking a cabinet works only if you always close the lock). Cut looped blind cords into separate strands to reduce the choking hazard or knot them up out of reach.

If you have glass-topped coffee tables, put them away, or put away any heavy objects that could be used to smash the glass (although you may be surprised—my first son smashed our glass-topped table

Mindful Mommy

Houseguests may not be as aware of childproofing as you are. Remind them to keep jewelry, makeup bags, shaving kits, and medications out of your baby's reach. Elderly guests, in particular, often don't keep their medication in childproof containers.

when he dropped a bongo drum onto it). Put away your tablecloth and invest in a set of place mats. If you sew, put your sewing basket up on a high shelf, and make sure you unplug your sewing machine and put it away every time you use it.

Make sure you can identify all your houseplants (if you have to, take a leaf to a local garden center) and confirm that they are nontoxic. Turn your water heater down to the lowest setting, if you haven't already. Put at least one trash can in a locked cabinet, and think before you throw things into accessible trash cans (avoid things like empty containers of cleaning products or used disposable razors).

Make a list of the childproofing gear you need to get. Don't buy everything in sight; you may be wasting your money, since some babies have no interest in toilets, doorstoppers, or stereo cords.

Start with stairs, which will probably need to be gated, as will any rooms that you plan to keep off limits. Gates that screw into the walls are better than pressure gates, particularly at the top of the stairs. You don't want a pressure gate giving way when your baby flings himself against it—and he will.

Mommy Must

Try making one room completely childproof, and put a gate on it. Then you can use it as a giant playpen when you need to contain your child.

You'll probably also want to get outlet covers—either caps for unused outlets or covers that block access to the plug for outlets you use frequently. You don't need cord shorteners—just use twist ties—and forget about cord guards and just use wide masking tape. Buy the more expensive type that is less likely to damage your paint. If your child is tall enough to reach the doorknobs, consider installing a chain or latch, high out of reach, on the doors that lead to the outside.

Additional Childproofing

- Remove or block access to furniture that is easily tipped over (like floor lamps)
- Regularly hunt for dropped coins or other potential choking hazards
- Do not use a baby walker anywhere around stairs
- Make sure your pool, if you have one, is solidly fenced and the gate is kept closed and locked. Hot tubs should be kept closed and locked when not in use, and toilets should be locked. Don't even leave a pail of water unattended.

Additional Childproofing for Cruisers and Walkers

- Install window guards if you live in an apartment or house with multiple floors
- Turn pot handles toward the back of the stove when cooking

- Make sure bookcases will not topple over
- Secure the TV so it won't fall if tugged on or pushed

Whether or not you need these items depends on the layout of your home and your childproofing decisions. For example, do you want to latch your kitchen cabinets or rearrange the contents so that all hazardous and breakable items are stowed high out of reach, and store only child-safe items (pots and pans, Tupperware) in the lower cabinets?

- ❏ Outlet covers or caps
- ❏ Gates
- ❏ Drawer and cabinet latches
- ❏ Toilet lock
- ❏ Foam strips or corners for table edges
- ❏ Window guards
- ❏ Window latches
- ❏ Oven lock
- ❏ Doorknob covers
- ❏ Stove knob covers

Double Checking
When you think you've thought of everything, watch your child to see what hazards she discovers. Is she fascinated by the oven door? You may have to strap it closed. Is she climbing the bookshelves? Make sure they are bolted to the wall. Some babies simply require more childproofing than others. You'll soon discover what kind of adventurer lives at your house.

Significant Dangers

Lead can be toxic to people of any age, but is particularly dangerous to young children. It damages the central nervous system, kidneys, and other organs and causes developmental delays, learning disabilities, and even permanent brain damage.

If your home was built before 1978, it may have been painted on the interior or exterior with lead-containing paint. On the interior, it may have several coats of safe paint over it, but it may chip (if, for example, your toddler rams his toy truck into a baseboard) or flake (as often happens when windows are raised and lowered). You may consider chemically stripping window areas and putting an extra coat of paint on areas that may chip. If the exterior was painted using lead-based paint, lead can seep into the surrounding ground. Have the soil tested before you let your child play in the dirt (and before you decide to plant a vegetable garden). Think twice about doing any renovation that disturbs old paint.

Lead can also be present in old pipes and can leach into the water. The local water department, upon request, may be willing to test your water free of charge; inexpensive test kits are also available. Also check certain brands of plastic blinds, ceramic dishes, and even some toys manufactured outside the United States with lead-check swabs, available at most hardware stores.

Baby walkers are another significant hazard for your baby. Simply put, infant walkers do not help babies walk. Besides being potentially dangerous—putting babies at risk of crashing into or reaching dangerous objects, like a hot stove, or tumbling down stairs—they can interfere with motor development. The reason: Walkers make it too easy for babies to get where they want to go and they don't experience the frustration that spurs the development of their motor skills. Babies need to see what they are doing as they try to figure out how to take their first steps, but in many styles of walkers, babies' feet are out of sight.

First Aid

As the parent of a small child, you'll be administering a lot of first aid—particularly once your child is getting around on her own. You can minimize hazards by childproofing, but your baby will still get her fair share of owies in her first year. Once your baby becomes mobile, you'll be patching up scrapes and bumps, pulling out splinters, and administering other forms of first aid. In addition to the usual

Mommy Knows Best

If you are concerned that your baby has already been exposed to high levels of lead, ask your doctor to perform a blood test. If the test does detect excessively high levels of lead, a medicine may be prescribed that can lower levels of lead stored in the body.

first aid supplies (like Band-Aids and sterile gauze), you'll need:

- First aid manual
- Telephone number for Poison Control
- Activated charcoal
- Adhesive tape
- Antiseptic wipes
- Papain (this natural meat tenderizer soothes bee stings)
- Antibiotic ointment such as Bacitracin
- Hydrocortisone cream
- Tweezers
- Calamine lotion
- Cold packs (instant, or keep one in the freezer; use a bag of frozen vegetables in a pinch)
- Cotton balls

It's also a good idea to keep scissors in your first aid kit (for cutting bandages and gauze strips), tweezers, and an old credit card for scraping bee stingers off the skin.

When to Go to the ER

Sometimes, a kiss, a Band-Aid, and an ice pack aren't enough. The following injuries may require immediate medical attention:

Head injuries:
- She vomits after the event
- She has a seizure

- The bleeding won't stop after five minutes of direct pressure
- He cries for more than ten minutes
- A severe fall (down a stairway, for example)
- He was/is unconscious, no matter how briefly
- His pupils are unequal in size

Also seek medical attention for cuts that are very deep or present a "smile" (the skin edges in the center of the cut are farther apart than on the ends) and for a burn if your baby's skin has blistering, significant swelling, white patches, or charring.

Chapter 13

Getting Around Town

BABIES ARE PORTABLE. THEY are easy to carry, will sleep just about anywhere, and don't beg to stop at McDonald's. Take advantage of it while you can, and take your baby on the road. Go out every day; your baby will thrive on exposure to new sights, sounds, and smells and you'll keep yourself from going nuts. You won't be this mobile for years to come.

Gearing Up for Travel

Babies don't much care where they're going when they go out, but moms tend to feel a little aimless without a destination. There are several destinations only a walk or short drive away available to most of us.

Stores are great places to take babies. Grocery stores, furniture stores, and book stores are all filled with brightly colored objects of various shapes, and people who love to smile at babies. Doors designed for wheelchair access are also stroller-friendly.

Go grocery shopping. Your infant car seat may be designed to clip safely to the seat of a shopping cart, or place it inside. Perhaps your local grocery store has special carts with built-in infant seats. (You may want to clean it with a baby wipe.) You can also shop with your baby in a frontpack or sling or, if you're only purchasing a few things, leave her in her stroller.

Go to the mall, indoor or outdoor. Talk to your baby about all the things you see. Admire the fountains and window shop; you don't have to actually buy anything. I was never more up to date on fashion trends than during my maternity leaves.

Consider a day at a museum. Call ahead and confirm that the museum you are considering visiting allows a baby backpack or a stroller; some don't allow them at all; some do on certain days. Front carriers and slings can pretty much go anywhere. When your baby is ready to eat, pick a bench in front of a painting you really like; if you're nursing, switch paintings when you switch breasts.

Be a tourist in your hometown. Big or small, your town probably has some tourist destinations locals are usually too busy to visit. If you live in a city, you probably already have your favorite spots to take visitors. Revisit them, and discover a few more.

Mindful Mommy

Stay away from clothing stores with narrow aisles and tightly packed racks. Your baby will end up with his face shoved into clothes, breathing chemicals (used to protect the fabric), gnawing on tags, and drooling on something you can't throw in the washer.

What You'll Need

Just as you prepared your home for an infant, travels with baby require very specific equipment. Do some research. Ask other new moms or your pediatrician for their recommendations, which might include the following:

- **Car seat:** Make sure your car seat model is up to date. Today's front-facing car seats include tether straps that attach to anchors that have been installed in all new vehicles since the model year 2001. Most cars made after 1989 have predrilled holes for tether anchors; ask your dealer to order the rest of the parts.
- **Stroller:** Strollers for infants should fully recline. If yours doesn't, borrow one that does or use a Snap-N-Go (a metal frame that converts your car seat into a stroller) until your baby can sit upright without slumping.
- **Jogging or off-road stroller:** A luxury item, unless you're a regular runner, but far easier to push on and off sidewalks when you're out for a long walk.
- **Rain cover for your stroller**
- **Sling and/or front carrier**
- **Baby backpack:** Once your baby can sit supported, these are better for long walks with a heavy baby than a frontpack.
- **Diaper bag or diaper backpack**
- **Portable crib or play yard:** Hotels will often supply cribs upon request, but these aren't

usually in the best condition. If you use one, measure the slats—they shouldn't be more than 2⅜ inches apart. If your baby isn't too mobile, you can put a dresser drawer on the floor and line it with a folded towel or two. Or bring a child's wading pool (it packs small and blows up easily; make sure it's firm when inflated) and line that with a towel or blanket.

- **Portable highchair:** If your baby is eating finger foods, a highchair will make mealtimes a lot more pleasant for everyone. We found that a clip-on highchair fit in the bottom of our biggest duffel bag.
- **Bike seat or bike trailer and helmet**

The more comprehensive your diaper bag, the less you'll end up buying on the road. Use your judgment, however, when buying accessories to pack in it. If the majority of your trips are to run errands or pick up older siblings, you may not need everything on this list. Pack the less-used items in a separate bag to keep with you for day trips and overnights.

- Diapers (at least four)
- A refillable pack of baby wipes
- Diaper rash ointment
- Plastic bags
- Light blanket (to cover your baby or use as a play mat)
- Waterproof changing pad or rubberized sheet

- Cloth diaper (for burping and general cleanup)
- Sunscreen (for babies over six months)
- Bottles and formula, unless you're nursing exclusively
- A snack for yourself and food for your older baby (Cheerios, etc.)
- Water bottle (for you to drink, and for cleanups)
- A change of clothes for you and your baby
- A stain-remover stick
- Travel pack of tissues
- A few toys or rattles

Prepack to prevent last-minute rushing—that's when you forget the essentials.

Dining Out

Take yourself out to lunch, breakfast, or dinner as often as you can when your baby is in the "luggage" stage (i.e., you can set her down anywhere and she doesn't move). Until your baby is eating solids, you don't even have to worry about selecting a child-friendly restaurant. You can actually eat at a restaurant that has tablecloths (but go early, it'll be less crazy and more fun). If your baby is hungry and you're nursing, toss a napkin over your shoulder and settle her in to feed; just order a meal that's not too hard to eat with one hand—avoid hot soup or coffee.

Choose a Child-Friendly Restaurant

Once your child can join you in a meal, pick a restaurant that caters to families. If your child is noisy, the other diners won't care as much, as you won't be interrupting romantic dates. The restaurant staff will be used to spills and the other children around will entertain your baby.

Signs you've found a family friendly restaurant:

- The table "linens" are really paper
- Your entrance went unremarked by the other diners and the patrons seated at tables near the door didn't turn around and stare
- Your child immediately sniffs out a toy box or play area
- The host or hostess doesn't look worried or panicked when you struggle in, loaded down with baby and gear
- Helium balloons are tied to the salad bar
- It's just noisy enough so you can't hear a spoon drop
- You see several families with kids and a big mess
- The hostess automatically picks up coloring sheets and crayons before leading you to your table
- More than one highchair is stacked in plain view
- You don't need to make a special request for a children's menu

When dining out anywhere, it will serve you well to bring along a few essentials to keep your baby entertained and allow you to enjoy your meal. Bring Cheerios or other finger foods and dole them out slowly, and bring a few small toys in case the finger foods lose their appeal.

Also, tip as heavily as you can. You'll be remembered for that, instead of for the mess you left in your wake.

Feeding an Older Baby

If you didn't pack dinner for your older baby, take a creative look at the menu. Do entrees come with vegetables? Maybe you can get a side order of steamed vegetables and cut them small or mash them. (It may take the kitchen two tries to cook the vegetables soft enough for a baby.) Are there eggs on the menu? Ask for scrambled eggs, yolks only. Is there a salad bar? Scavenge it for soft fruits and vegetables you can cut into bite-sized pieces. Most chefs can quickly prepare a dish of plain pasta.

At the Movies

Try taking your baby to the movies. Catch an afternoon matinee, when the theaters are nearly empty or

Mommy Knows Best

When dining out with your baby, it helps to place your order as quickly as you can, and when the food arrives, ask for the check; you may make it through dinner with a contented baby, only to have him melt down during a long wait for the bill.

an evening show on a weeknight. Pick an aisle seat, just in case you need to bolt—but the odds are that you won't. Theaters are dark, and after nursing or drinking a bottle, your baby is likely to go to sleep. If not, he may kick back and watch the show. Or bring quiet cloth toys and teethers (leave the rattles at home). This is not, however, the time to pick an action movie that amplifies tire squeals and gunshots in full digital surround sound. Go for a chick flick— lots of dialog and close ups of faces (which babies love). My youngest was a regular at my monthly movie group until he was nearly ten months old.

Theaters in some towns even encourage parents to bring babies to special showings where fussing is allowed.

Hiking, Biking, Camping, and More

If you like to hike, you don't have to give it up now; if you never were a hiker, this may be the time to start (but begin with short, easy trails). Stay out of constant sun (don't forget your baby's hat) and avoid trails with low branches. Use a frontpack until your baby is too heavy for one, then switch to a backpack.

Or just walk around town. Admire your neighbors' gardens, get to know the neighborhood pets by name, and go out for an evening walk with a flashlight for extra baby entertainment.

What about parks and playgrounds? They're a great place to meet other moms, but save them for after your baby is sitting or crawling and can take advantage of the swings and sandbox. Until then, pick outings that interest you more; you'll be getting plenty of playground time over the next few years.

Biker Baby

After your baby is able to hold up and control her head for extended periods of time (usually at around nine months), she's ready to experience life in the bike lane. Get a helmet that fits her well (make sure it has a gently rounded, not flared, back, or she won't be able to lean her head back comfortably) and a bike seat (make sure the seat keeps her feet away from the wheels) or a trailer.

Car Travel

Some babies seem to fall asleep the minute they feel the car's motor start; others scream. The problem with car travel for some babies seems to be boredom. For a very young baby, pictures to look at may help. Prop a book or a plastic picture holder designed for the car on the seat facing your baby or try hanging a mirror designed for crib use from the back headrest so your baby can admire himself. Company in the back seat or

Mommy Must

Don't limit your walks to balmy spring days. Try rain walks. If your baby is in a frontpack, sling, or backpack, an umbrella will protect both of you, and your baby will be fascinated by the sound and smell of rain.

music also keep your baby content. Bring toys for older babies; hook them to the car seat with plastic links, or they'll all end up on the floor in minutes. Stopping—to change a diaper or soothe the baby—usually doesn't help, unless you're planning a long stop.

Packing for Vacation

When packing all of your baby care essentials for vacation, it's important to plan ahead and know what you must bring and what you can purchase at your destination. Besides clothes for your baby, you'll need:

- ❏ Car seat
- ❏ Stroller
- ❏ Food for trip, including powdered formula and water, if you're bottle-feeding
- ❏ Diapers and wipes (bring enough for two days; buy the rest at your destination)
- ❏ A favorite toy
- ❏ New toy for trip
- ❏ Portable crib, sheets, favorite blanket
- ❏ Portable highchair
- ❏ CDs of music if you'll be traveling by car
- ❏ Baby-proofing gadgets (If your baby is crawling, baby-proof at least one room at your destination. Bring a pack of outlet covers and a few cabinet locks.)
- ❏ Your medical insurance card and doctor's phone number
- ❏ First aid kit
- ❏ Sunscreen

If you're going on a long trip, try to plan the trip around your baby's regular sleep schedule. Figure that she might be happily awake in the car seat for as much as an hour—but not much more. If you leave an hour before naptime, she'll be awake for an hour, and fall asleep, if you're lucky, for two hours. Then stop to feed her, change her, maybe eat dinner yourself, and get her back in the car for another hour awake and hope that brings you to your destination. If your baby is hungry, don't remove her from her car seat while the car is in motion; stop to nurse.

The best news about car travel is that children under the age of two rarely suffer from motion sickness. This particular treat may be in your future, but is not something you have to deal with right now.

Into the Woods

You can go camping with an infant, although you may have to pack a few more things than you are used to. Along with your regular camping gear, consider bringing:

- A waterproof crib pad for inside your sleeping bag, if you're sleeping with your baby
- A portable crib, if you're not
- An inflatable wading pool for use as bathtub and/or a crib
- A large plastic bin to pack your clothes in and use as a tub to wash your baby
- An extra warm sleeper

- A blanket for sitting on when you are outside the tent
- A highchair if your baby is eating finger foods (it will give him a chance to get the food in his mouth before it gets covered with dirt, and can be used to contain him when you don't want to worry about him crawling into the fire)

If you're hiking with your baby in a backpack, it's worthwhile to also bring a makeup mirror in your pocket. Pull it out to use as a rear-view mirror to check on your baby.

Remember to check out your campsite completely before letting your baby loose, in case previous campers left things behind that you don't want your baby to put in her mouth.

Beach Baby

I'm a beach person, so the first place I think of taking an infant on vacation is a tropical beach. All three of my kids were in the ocean before they could crawl and took long afternoon naps under beach umbrellas.

If you are planning a day—or longer—at the beach with your baby, be sure you protect him from the sun. While chemical sunblocks don't seem to have any negative effects on young babies, you may want to try one that uses zinc or titanium oxide, which provide physical rather than chemical blocks. Patch test any sunscreen before covering your baby with it. Put a dab on the inside of your baby's arm and cover it with a Band-Aid. Check the skin after twenty minutes and again after twenty-four hours. You're looking for red blotches or bumps. If you see them, cross that brand off your list.

Also, dress your baby in lightweight cotton clothes that cover her arms and legs. Use a hat with a brim that goes all the way around and sunglasses. She may not keep them on, but she may love them. If she does, you'll be protecting her from long-term eye damage and short-term crankiness—bright sun glaring off of water may make her uncomfortable. You can also invest in special UV clothes that are lightweight and sunproof even when wet.

- Bring or rent an umbrella and keep him in the shade as much as possible. Consider getting off the beach altogether in the middle of the day.
- Bring extra T-shirts. Leave a shirt on when your baby is splashing in the water to protect her from the sun, and change it when she's done.
- Bring (and remember to drink) extra fluids, so you and your baby stay properly hydrated.

Mindful Mommy

If your baby's old enough to hang on to a toy, bring a bucket and shovel. She may not know how to play with them yet, but she'll love it when you demonstrate water dumping and castle building. Her job at this point is to knock your castles down.

- Use cornstarch or cornstarch-based baby powder to remove sand—it works better than water.

One thing you don't want to forget: Bring lots of regular diapers or swim diapers. Swim diapers pull on like training pants and, because they don't contain the superabsorbent gels of regular diapers, won't immediately fill up with water and explode. They contain poop pretty well, but do less well with pee. Too much time in a wet diaper can kick off a bout of diaper rash, so you will need to change your baby often.

While you'll want to dip your baby's toes in the water, don't take him all the way into the ocean or a pool until he can support his head on his own. The water temperature ought to be fairly warm—above 84°F—to prevent hypothermia. You shouldn't keep your baby in the water longer than half an hour; even water that warm will eventually chill your child.

In a pool, go ahead and use a tube specially designed for a baby (with straps between the legs) or a life vest, but don't consider these as replacements

Mommy Knows Best

Your baby will probably taste the sand and may eat handfuls of it. Don't worry, it will simply go through her digestive system and she'll eventually pass it.

for your arms—stay within reach. A baby can slip from a tube or tip face first into the water when wearing a vest.

Taking to the Skies

There is nothing that instills panic in the minds of parents—as well as other passengers and flight attendants—as the thought of a baby's first airplane trip. It can be rough. Actually, it can be horrible. Your baby may scream for hours, throw up all over you, and leak through her last dry set of clothes (been there, done that, and wouldn't even talk about getting on a plane for the next six months). Or your baby may sleep the whole way and wake only as the plane is coming in for a landing.

While traveling with an infant may be rough on parents, it isn't, under normal circumstances, hazardous to the baby. There is no clear medical reason to forego air travel until an infant is a certain age, although some airlines have restrictions on travel for infants only a few days old. Unless a trip is critical, you might consider holding off until your baby is more than two months old; airplanes tend to be germ-rich places, and when a baby under two months old gets a fever for any reason, it is a concern.

When you make your reservations, think about your child's temperament at different times of the day. If he fusses every evening and needs to be walked for hours, a late-day flight is probably not a good idea.

227

If he typically falls asleep easily and sleeps all night, maybe you're a candidate for a red-eye. This is a risky move, though; fellow passengers who will grin and bear it when a baby is crying on a daytime flight can get downright nasty when their sleep is interrupted by a crying baby.

A Seat of Her Own

Consider purchasing a seat for your baby. Yes, she can fly free (or, on international flights, for a small fee), and the extra cost may be prohibitive, but having a guaranteed spot for your baby's car seat can make the difference between a merely stressful flight and torture. You can put her down if she falls asleep, for one, and be able to lower your tray table and eat something yourself. It's also a lot safer. Ask—it probably won't cost as much as your ticket and many carriers have greatly reduced fares for children under two.

If you do purchase a seat, make sure to reserve the window for your baby; you won't be allowed to use the car seat in any other seat as it may block access to the aisle. You can also request a baby meal. Most airlines offer this option, which is usually a few jars of baby food.

Know What to Ask For

If you aren't purchasing an extra seat and are traveling with another adult or child, ask for an aisle and a window seat when you make your reservations. If you're lucky, the center seat will remain unoccupied.

If not, whoever is assigned that seat will be happy to switch for your aisle or window and may, if your baby starts fussing before takeoff, look for a seat far away. (Hint: Boarding is not the time to worry about quieting your baby; you want to clear your row.) You may have been advised to ask for a bulkhead row. This tip makes sense, but unless you or your traveling companion is a high-mileage flier, forget about it; most airlines award bulkhead seats to good customers, not families with kids.

Try to get a seat in the front third of the airplane. Some airplanes have been remodeled to give front passengers extra leg room, and those few inches may make the difference between whether you can wriggle down to pick up a dropped rattle or not. If the front third is booked, try for one of the last few rows. You'll be close to the bathroom and at least have some floor space to pace with your baby.

Travel Tips

- Gate-check your stroller. Tell the person checking boarding passes that you want a gate-check; he'll give you a special tag. Then you can push

Mindful Mommy

When planning trips that include your baby, try to make airline reservations for his least fussy time of day.

your baby all the way down the boarding ramp and unload your stroller just outside the door to the airplane. It will be returned to you as you leave the airplane at your destination and will make it a lot easier to get your baby and his gear to the baggage area.

- Bring a car seat aboard. (Make sure that it's no wider than fifteen inches—that means it will fit in most coach seats.) You may also have to prove that your car seat is FAA approved; if it doesn't say so on the label, it may in the instruction manual. Some infant seats will fit in the overhead compartment; if yours does, and you don't have a seat reserved for your baby, stash it there as soon as you get it on the plane.

- If you are using a convertible car seat (the kind that can be strapped in the rear-facing position for infants and switched to front-facing for older children), you may have to strap it in the front-facing position to fit it on the airplane. This isn't ideal, but it's safer than your lap.

- Bring plenty of extra formula. Plane travel is dehydrating. If you're using powdered formula, bring plenty of water. (I'll never forget the time I asked a flight attendant repeatedly for water for my son's bottle and was eventually shooed over to the bathroom and told to help myself at the tap. I did, and was shaking the bottle to mix the formula when I noticed the label above the sink: "Water nonpotable.")

- Preboarding. It's easier to get yourself and your gear stowed, strapped in, and settled before hordes of anxious passengers are trying to cram past you. Unfortunately, this courtesy is offered less and less often. If there isn't an announcement, ask if you can preboard; some airlines will respond to individual requests. If you're traveling as a solo parent with a baby, beg. Groveling is better than being trampled by impatient passengers as you are trying to stow your gear without dropping your baby.
- Nurse or feed your baby during takeoff and landing. The sucking and swallowing helps prevent discomfort in her ears from the changes in air pressure. If she's sleeping during takeoff, let her sleep; but if she's sleeping during landing, wake her up, that's when the pressure is the worst. If she's not interested in eating, use an eyedropper to put drops of water, juice, or milk in her mouth. She'll swallow them, and the swallowing will clear her ears. (Screaming will clear her ears, too, of course.)
- Drink plenty of fluids yourself. Bring a sport water bottle and get it refilled; it's easier to manage while wrestling a baby than a plastic cup or soda can. This is critical if you are nursing. Again, air travel is extremely dehydrating; if you're not careful, your milk supply can be depleted for a day or two.

- Bring extra clothes. Your baby is not the only one who is going to get messy if he throws up or has a diaper blowout. Keep a change of clothes for yourself and plastic grocery bags for the mess in your carry-on.
- Bring a favorite toy or two. Be on the lookout for found toys, too. The laminated card with the picture of emergency exits somehow fascinates babies, and you can make puppets out of air-sickness bags.

Induced Sleep?

Some moms credit over-the-counter antihistamines (usually Benadryl or an equivalent) for ensuring that their babies spend most of their plane trips dozing. However, about 10 percent of children react in a paradoxical way to antihistamines and end up speedy instead of drowsy. If you're thinking about trying it, check the dosage with your doctor and do a test run at home.

If you'd like a more peaceful baby, but don't want to resort to antihistamines, try a bottle of chamomile tea. My breastfeeding babies, who never wanted anything to do with bottles of breastmilk or formula, were usually willing to drink this on an airplane. Brew it before you leave, adding a teaspoon of sugar to about three-quarters of a cup of hot tea, and pour it into a bottle. It'll be lukewarm when you're on board.

Other Travel Challenges

Finding a place to change a diaper on an airplane is a challenge. Forget about the bathrooms; only rarely will you get a plane with a fold-down changing table, and the ones that exist are so small as to be practically useless. The bathrooms themselves have no counter space and the floors are typically wet and sticky.

If you have a row to yourself, change your baby on your seats. Smile apologetically to nearby passengers if it's a smelly diaper and whisk it into the airsick bag as quickly as possible. Speed is important here.

If you don't have a row to yourself, your best bet is to change your baby on the floor at the back of the plane. Try to crouch out of the path of anyone who might walk by, and put a blanket or two on the floor before you spread out your changing pad (again, the floor is likely to be pretty yucky). Or, you can punt on the issue by slathering your baby's bottom with diaper cream and putting a superabsorbent diaper or double diapers on her just before boarding and hope she doesn't poop before landing.

If you're switching planes as a solo parent and can't figure out how you are going to race with your baby, car seat, and diaper bag from gate to gate, try calling the airline. You may be able to arrange for help in the form of a chauffeured electric cart.

Mommy Must

Always keep small plastic grocery bags with you. They are perfect for collecting and properly disposing of dirty diapers and used wipes.

International Trips

If you're planning to travel internationally, give yourself plenty of time to get a passport for your baby. Getting a passport photo for an infant can be tricky. The instant cameras used for passport photos in photo shops don't work well with babies because they are designed to focus best at a distance of about four feet, and getting an infant's head to fill the photo requires getting in closer. Some photographers won't even try to produce passport photos of children under two. If you want to try the photo shop, bring a white blanket and an infant seat. The passport agency does not want your face in there with your baby's, and the photographer will have a better chance of getting a usable shot if your baby is comfortable, rather than being held in your hands at an awkward distance from your body.

You don't actually have to use an official passport photo. The shot needs to be taken head on, and your baby's eyes should be open. The background should be white or very light. You need two identical photos that are at least two inches square; the face, from the

Mommy Knows Best

When traveling internationally, be sure all of your documentation is in order. In addition to passports for you and your baby, bring copies of your birth and marriage certificates.

top of the head to the bottom of the chin, should measure between one and 1⅜ inches.

So get out your ruler and scissors and start measuring photos. If you bought photos from the hospital photographer, try the wallet-sized prints—with some judicious trimming, these very well may work. Otherwise, lay your baby on a white blanket and stand over him (you may want to use a stool), taking shots from varying distances in hopes that one will be the right size.

In addition to your passports, bring a copy of your baby's birth certificate and your marriage certificate; they may come in handy. If you are traveling without your spouse, bring a letter from him giving you permission to take your baby out of the country and have a phone number where he can be contacted.

If you have the option, pick a foreign airline. They tend to be more baby friendly than U.S.-based airlines. International flights often accommodate bassinets—special little beds that go on the floor or attach to a bulkhead. Reserve one ahead of time; they are usually free of charge, but may be in limited supply.

If you are packing baby formula, make sure it is unopened. Pack formula for the plane ride separately. Otherwise, you may not be able to bring it in the country. Be sure to declare it, if asked.

Charts and Tables

Food Introduction Record

Food	Date of Introduction	Likes/ Dislikes	Allergic Reaction (Describe)
SIX MONTHS (ONE MEAL A DAY)			
Rice cereal			
Banana			
Avocado			
Applesauce			
Apple juice			
Oat cereal			
Squash			
Pears			
Wheat cereal			
Pear juice			
Sweet potatoes			
SEVEN MONTHS (ONE TO TWO MEALS A DAY)			
Barley cereal			
Peaches			
Carrots			
Plums			
Peas			
Prune juice			

Food Introduction Record (continued)

EIGHT MONTHS (TWO TO THREE MEALS A DAY)

Chicken

Green beans

Grape juice

Turkey

Papaya juice

NINE MONTHS (THREE MEALS A DAY)

Beef

TEN MONTHS (THREE MEALS A DAY)

Tofu

Oranges

Orange juice

Lamb

Broccoli

Grapefruit

Beets

ELEVEN MONTHS (THREE MEALS A DAY)

Egg yolks

Spinach

Kiwi

Potatoes

The one rule you should follow: Wait at least three days after
introducing a new food, adding it in small portions along with
foods already allergy tested, before adding another new one.
Should you follow this order exactly, you'll find you'll alter-
nate the introduction of new fruits, vegetables, cereals, and
proteins.

Health History

Information you and anyone else taking care of your baby will need to have on hand. Start keeping track of it now.

Date of birth, name of hospital, doctors:

_____

Weight, length, head size:

_____

Any congenital problems:

_____

_____

_____

Complications during pregnancy or delivery:

_____

_____

_____

How long breastfed:

_____

_____

_____

Health History (continued)

Food allergies:

_____

_____

Drug allergies:

_____

_____

Chronic conditions (frequent ear infections, asthma,
other):

_____

_____

Major medical treatments (surgeries or
hospitalizations):

_____

_____

Vaccinations:

_____

_____

_____

Illnesses:

_____

_____

Date of onset:

_____

_____

Date of recovery:

_____

_____

Diagnosis:

_____

_____

Medications given:

_____

_____

Reactions to medication:

_____

_____

Common Vaccinations

There has been a lot of talk about vaccines recently, and it is easy to get confused by the different opinions from various mothers, doctors, friends, and family members. Here's a list that will familiarize you with the vaccines that most doctors recommend. But, as always, consult with your pediatrician about what is right for your baby!

- **Diphtheria:** An infection of the tonsils and upper airway that can interfere with breathing and cause heart problems and paralysis.
- **Tetanus:** An infection from contaminated wounds that shuts down the central nervous system.
- **Pertussis:** Also called whooping cough, an infection that is characterized by a cough so bad that it can lead to convulsions or choking.
- **H influenza type B (HIB):** An infection that is the leading cause of meningitis, which can cause permanent brain damage.
- **Polio:** A viral infection that can cause permanent paralysis.
- **Measles:** A rash disease that can lead to brain damage or blindness.
- **Mumps:** A virus in which the salivary glands swell; severe cases can lead to meningitis, hearing loss, or, in boys, sterility.
- **Hepatitis B:** An infection of the liver that can cause liver cancer or liver failure.
- **Chicken pox or varicella:** Another rash disease, with pimple-like spots, usually mild in children, although it can cause scarring. In severe cases, it can be fatal. (The American Academy of Pediatrics recommends this relatively new vaccine, so consult your pediatrician. Some parents prefer to expose their

children to the disease instead, believing that will provide stronger lifelong immunity.)

Typical Vaccination Schedule

Your doctor's vaccination recommendations may vary, and these schedules change regularly.

Hepatitis B:	Birth, one month, six-eighteen months
Diphtheria, Tetanus, Pertussis:	Two months, four months, six months, twelve-eighteen months
H. Influenza type B:	Yearly starting at 6 months
Polio:	Two months, four months, six-eighteen months
Measles, Mumps, Rubella:	Twelve months, four-six years
PCV (Pneumococcal):	Two months, four months, six months, twelve-eighteen months

My Baby's Milestones

Use the following section to record you baby's milestones. Use extra paper if you'd like.

Claps: _____

Grabs a toy or object: What?_____

Rolls over: _____

Sits unsupported:_____

Crawls, creeps, or somehow crosses the room:_____

Pulls up to a stand:_____

On what? _____

Walks: _____

How many steps? _____

Climbs out of crib: _____

Runs: _____

Smiles: _____

At what? _____

Laughs out loud: _____

At what? _____

Shows excitement: _____

At what? _____

Shows anger: _____

At what? _____

Has a favorite toy: _____

What is it? _____

Coos or oohs (vowels): _____

What did it sound like? _____

Babbles (consonants): _____

What sounds are the favorites? _____

Babbles without repeating syllables: _____

What did it sound like? _____

First word: _____

Word? _____

Second word: _____

Word? _____

First animal sound: _____

What animal? _____

List all the words your baby can say on his or her first birthday:

_____

_____

_____

_____

_____

Index